DADDY SET THE CHURCH ON FIRE

A JOURNEY TOWARD RESTORATION

MICHAEL CHARLES OLSON

FOREWORD BY: MICHAEL W. SMITH

BRIDGE LOGOS
Newberry, FL 32669

Bridge-Logos, Inc.
Newberry, FL 32669

Daddy Set the Church on Fire
by Michael Olson

Printed in the United States of America.

Library of Congress Catalog Card Number: 2025943886

International Standard Book Number: 978-1-61036-921-3

Cover Design and Illustrations | Joshua Noom

Interior Layout and Design
Ashley Morgan | GraphicGardenLLC@gmail.com

Edited by Julie Klose | JulieKlose.com

I thank God for my brother and friend Michael Olson. From the first day we sat across that table at Angie's Subs in Jacksonville, I could see a man marked by both wounds and worship. I've watched him walk through seasons of deep pain and even deeper redemption, and I've seen Jesus use every scar to shape a shepherd's heart that burns for the glory of God and the good of His Church.

Daddy Set the Church on Fire is more than a story—it's a testimony of what happens when a son learns to see his life through the eyes of the Father. Michael doesn't just write about restoration; he lives it. Every page carries the weight of a man who has wrestled with grace, fatherhood, failure, and faith—and found Jesus faithful through it all.

I've had the privilege of serving alongside Michael, and I can say this without hesitation: the same Holy Spirit who lights up these pages is the One who lights up his life. If you've ever wondered whether God can redeem the ashes of your past and set your heart ablaze again, this book will show you He can—and He does.

—Pastor Joby Martin,
Lead Pastor, The Church of Eleven22

Michael has penned a poignantly-powerful remembrance of a father who shared the gift of music with his son only to bury deep wounds beneath the melodies. A magnificently-gifted musician, and tormented addict, Michael's dad spiraled into despondency eventually setting their house on fire burning everything they owned to the ground. Raised in the ashes, Michael would grow into a powerfully talented singer and songwriter, traveling the world and performing before hundreds of thousands. And yet when the lights dimmed and applause faded, Michael would not escape the sins of his father. Confused, wounded and angry, Michael lived out of one half of a broken heart, wrestling daily the damaging ripple effects of unforgiveness, and the exponential pain of betrayal. And right there in the middle of that mess is where Jesus met Michael. And when He did, He brought with Him an unexpected redemption, an impossible reconciliation and a freedom despite the scars. This is a hauntingly-honest, soul-inside-out story, which reminds us that there is no pain and no wound that the incomparable and inconceivable love of God can not only heal but make all things new.

—Charles Martin,
New York Times Bestselling Author

Michael Olson is, without question, one of the most talented people I've ever known. That's saying a lot, considering I've spent more than 32 years in the Christian music industry and ministry and have had the privilege of knowing many remarkably gifted musicians. I first met Michael years ago while touring with my band Third Day alongside our mentor and friend Michael W. Smith. It didn't take long to realize that Michael wasn't just an exceptionally skilled multi-instrumentalist and vocalist—he is also a remarkable songwriter.

Beyond his musical abilities, Michael is a genuinely kind and compassionate human being who truly cares for others. And just when I think I've exhausted all the ways I can be jealous of his talent, I pick up his book... and discover he's an outstanding author too!

I know you'll be encouraged, as I have been, by Michael's storytelling—rooted in heart, humor, and honesty. His reflections have deeply resonated with me, especially as someone who shares the experience of having a meaningful yet complicated relationship with my own departed father.

Enjoy this wonderful debut book from my friend Michael. I'm confident it's only the first of many beautiful works he'll share with us in the years ahead.

—Mac Powell,
Multiple Grammy Award Winning Artist

I first met Michael at my breakfast table. Within fifteen minutes, we were deep in one of the most honest and profound conversations about life, worship, and the church. A day or two later, it felt like we had known each other forever, sharing wounded pasts and a similar journey toward redeemed fatherhood. That conversation—and that friendship—has never really stopped.

This book is exactly that: an uninterrupted, real-life conversation with a friend; an open invitation to redemption and forgiveness in the most formative relationship a boy will ever have—his relationship with his father. It's also a testimony of fatherhood restored by the grace of the Father whose relentless pursuit of His children never ends.

Michael and I have both lived this story. He's simply more gifted storyteller than I am—and rightly so! Just be warned: give him fifteen minutes, and you may walk away with a lifelong friend. I'm grateful I did.

—Rafal Piekarski,
Lead Pastor of Tomy Christian Fellowship,
Proem Ministries Poland

Michael's book is a gift—a deeply personal and profoundly theological exploration of forgiveness that resonates far beyond its pages. As a pastor, theologian, artist, and worship leader, Michael brings a rare blend of intellect and authenticity to this work. Over the years, I've had the privilege of countless conversations with him about God, life, stewardship, and fatherhood—especially in the sacred context of raising our boys. His wisdom and humility have always left me inspired, and this book captures that same spirit.

A deep thinker, probing his own journey, Michael illuminates the transformative power of forgiveness, not just as an individual act but as a generational calling—a bridge toward reconciliation that heals families and restores legacies. This is not theory; it is lived truth, written by a man who has wrestled deeply and emerged with grace. If you long for hope, healing, and a vision of what redemption can look like through the empowerment of forgiveness, this book will speak to your soul.

"Forgiveness isn't just for today—it's the key to healing generations."

—Asher Chanan-Khan, MD
Professor of Medicine,
Mayo Clinic

I have the great pleasure of being led in worship by Michael each week, and having this glimpse into who he is and where he came from has meant so much. His hope in Jesus is real, and it's infectious. In *Daddy Set the Church on Fire*, Michael reminds us that in Jesus there is hope and healing for the wounded spirit who has watched everything familiar burn to the ground. His pastoral heart can be seen on every page as he reveals how God meets us to redeem the ashes. If you need to be reminded that Jesus makes all things new, this is the book!

—Lysa TerKeurst,
#1 New York Times Bestselling Author and President of Proverbs 31 Ministries

---

My last couple of decades have been better because of my dear friend Michael. He has been a living parable to me of what it looks like to worship the Lord in spirit and truth.

I have had a front row seat to walking with a brother who has an unusual pairing of a deep love for biblical truth and a crazy emotional capacity to feel it. This combo makes Michael an incredible writer. Now you get to pull up a chair to experience Michael's journey of brokenness to restoration in Jesus as he wraps words around the movements of grace that compel the heart to burst forth in songs of praise. I am praying that God would use these pages to inspire you to take hold of the life of freedom that Jesus has already purchased for you on the cross.

—Shane Barnard,
1/2 of Shane and Shane and songwriter

FOR BRODY,
BENTLEY,
AND BECKETT

Boys,
Don't ever give away your innocence
Don't trade the mystery for common sense
Guard your hearts
True,
In time, I'll grow to know the men you'll be
But somewhere deep inside the heart of me
You'll be boys

—Michael Olson

From the song "Boys", Heartland

FOREWORD

I feel very fortunate to have had the opportunities I've had. I commonly use the phrase "It's been a wild ride" to describe the journey the Lord has led me on over the years. Looking back, I can honestly say that one of the most meaningful parts of it has been the deep friendships I've made along the way. Particularly the people that I've been able to share life with on the road. There's a certain kind of camaraderie that comes with midnight bus calls, mad dashes through airports, and belly laughs around pre-show catering dinner tables. Some things push these friendships to an even deeper place. Things like side-stage prayer meetings, vulnerable conversations in the back lounge of tour buses, and moments when eyes and hearts lock while leading people all over the world in the worship of Jesus. They are treasures. I had the great blessing of sharing moments like these with Michael Olson. I simply call him *"O."*

It's crazy to think that *"O"* was born the same year I signed my first songwriting contract. He's told me stories of his older brother bringing him to Michael W. Smith arena shows in the suburbs of Chicago when he was in junior high. I suppose one of the reasons why that strikes me as being so strange is the instant brotherhood we experienced when we started playing music together, so many years later. First, in the context of the small church that was planted out of a Bible study that met in the barn at my farm. Then . . . all over the world.

I signed Michael O. as an artist on Rocketown Records and asked him to play drums on the road with me. We spent six years together. During that time, we discovered that we were kindred spirits, mutually encouraging each other in the pursuit of serving Jesus and His bride as leaders of worship. It's a beautiful thing to create a sound with a brother like that. A sound that inspires people to sing what they think and feel about Jesus *to* Jesus, only to back away in silence, and hear them take over. To take your fingers off the keys, to put the drumsticks down, and hear people from all over the world sing together in unison. I still love it.

While song was the method we used to lead worship in public, we also both shared the desire to see God worshiped in the ins and outs of our everyday lives. For me, that has looked like being an honoring son to Paul and Barbara, a faithful husband to Debbie, and a present father to Ryan, Whitney, Tyler, Anna, and Emily–not to mention all the grandkids who have followed. This sort of thing doesn't always come as easily as songs do. It's incredibly rewarding, but it's often complicated and requires a great deal of investment and sacrifice.

Here's the thing–at this stage in my journey, I can clearly see the beauty and necessity of God's work in these areas and how they inform the worship song that's sung in public. Without a doubt, Paul Smith's investment in me as a loving father was primary in shaping my understanding of God's father heart. I've been known to talk about it from the stage . . . *"My dad thinks I hung the moon."* He passed away in November of 2015, but it's still true to this day. I've felt the weight of it as I've fathered my own kids, particularly in my relationships with my two boys, Ryan and Tyler. I've felt the importance of getting it right as best I can. It's a massive responsibility.

What you're about to read in this book is how this has played out in Michael O's life. It's how God has shaped him as a son, a husband, a father, a friend, and ultimately . . . *a worshiper*. I've had a front row seat to some of it. Some of the vulnerable back lounge bus conversations we shared were about the complexity of his relationship with his dad. He struggled to make sense of it in real time as we shared life together on the road. I listened. I saw firsthand the way he loved Ashley, his beautiful, Canadian wife. They had their first son, Brody, induced a week early so Michael could be at home for a few days before we jumped into a Spring touring run. In fact, the reason he decided to get off the road with me was to spend more time at home after Brody was born. I remember he and Ashley carrying his tiny, newborn frame onto the bus and laying him down on his bunk. Michael's drumsticks were longer than Brody, all stretched out from head to toe. *"O"* had a glimmer in his eye as he looked down at him. I knew the feeling.

God is at work in these areas of our lives. They make us the worshippers we are. The songs we sing are built on the foundation of His faithfulness in every season, and His ability to redeem what's broken and heal what's hurt. It's a part of this wonderful journey of abundant life that

He's got us on. I'm excited and prayerful for you as you turn these pages. Warning: some of it is not for the faint of heart, but it's all true. My prayer is that as you go on "O's" journey, you'll discover God's redemptive work on your own, and that the discovery will spill out in songs of gratitude and adoration like they have for him.

—Michael W. Smith
Multiple Grammy Award
Winning Recording Artist

AUTHOR'S NOTE

Childhood is a gift from God. Boyhood is the version of childhood that I'm most familiar with, as I had some experience with it for a short period of time. I am also a father. I have three boys of my own, whom I can only hope will enjoy boyhood for as long as they possibly can. Maybe they will even carry some version of it with them as they grow and mature into the men they will become. Everyone knows that boys become men, and some men become fathers who raise kids of their own. Half of these will be boys, continuing the cycle.

Life is transformation. More specifically, the Christian life is transformation into the image of Christ. There is no greater transformation that one can experience. However, be aware that this journey is not for the faint of heart. Boys fall and end up with scraped knees, and men stumble and end up with wounded souls. All of this affects who they are and who they raise as they participate in the cycle of boys becoming men becoming fathers. It doesn't always go as expected.

In the journey of transformation into the image of Christ, who happens to be a Son with a Father himself, there will be death . . . and death is painful. Even the most sanctified version of it. For all the talk of boys being born for war, making swords out of sticks and handguns out of anything with a right angle (which is true), boyhood is a fragile thing. For the vast majority of men, it's looked back on and longed for. On the rare occasion that we men are honest with ourselves, we discover that we are fragile, too. I think if you took the time to sit and look a hundred men in the eye for five minutes and ask them about their boyhood, a hundred of them would have a memory or two that would bring a smile to their face. They would also have one or two that would take that smile away. Without a doubt, there's some correlation between the level of internal equilibrium these men demonstrate and the memories they share.

I know men who lost their boyhood too quickly, making their journey into manhood and fatherhood more complicated. I know one of them well. I see him in the mirror every morning. "Old soul" is the term we use to describe these people. On the surface, it's complimentary, as *you are smarter than you should be*. But something lies beneath the compliment. Something dark and sinister. It sounds more like: *How did you end up like this?* It can also be asked introspectively, as in: *How did I end up like this?* That sounds worse. Heads up, it's a question that all men will ask of themselves at some point, maybe even in the middle of trying to raise sons of their own.

Answering that question forces you to confront the journey you've been on. You're not just where you are, but also where you've been. Madeleine L'Engle said, "I am still every age that I have been." It's true, for better and for worse. Springtime possibilities, summer blossoming, and the harsh reality of what comes with fall's impending frost all play into it. Here's the good news, and I use the words "good news" on purpose. Where you are and where you've been do not define who you are or who you will become. That reality is tied up in something else, or *Someone* else, altogether.

I want to tell you a story. It's a true story. In my opinion, true stories are the best kind. Here's why: Although true stories have to do with the people, places, joys, and wounds we have experienced personally, they point us to something beyond ourselves. More accurately said, they point us to *Someone* beyond ourselves. That is certainly the case with this one. True stories have an author, and it's not us. What you're about to read is my true story. It's the way I've experienced the Author's work in my life personally, as a boy who, through life's twists and turns, grew into a man who became a husband and a father.

I'll present the story in three parts, like a classic Shakespearean play. Each part tells the story of a musical instrument that is near and dear to me. What I find surprising is that while each part tells the story of the instrument, it simultaneously points to a broader redemption narrative that unfolds in a unique and allegorical way. I hope that as you read my story, you will discover something about your own, and who and where you are in the midst of it.

To that end, I've included a guided reflection and prayer section at the end of each of the three parts. As you read and reflect on my story, you might be spurred on to see how the Author is redemptively at work in your own. You should also know that the end of my story hasn't been written yet. I'm still in the process. The same can be said for you. I'm confident that the way our stories wrap up will have a lot to do with what has happened in them so far. There won't be any wasted words. The more time passes, the more I become familiar with the heart of the Author. He's a great storyteller.

PROLOGUE

I have memories of the simplicity and innocence of boyhood. Many that bring a smile to my face involve my closest boyhood friend, Jimmy Nichols. His name might as well have been Eddy Haskell from the iconic television sitcom *Leave It to Beaver*. Jimmy was the youngest child of the Reverend Jim Nichols, the associate pastor of Northwest Assembly of God, the charismatic Pentecostal church where we grew up. Besides his mom and dad, Jimmy lived with his two elder sisters. Their entire family's first names were often stated together in rapid-fire fashion: Jim (dad), Jill (mom), Julie (older sister), Joy (middle sister), and Jimmy.

Jimmy bore the characteristics of a true pastor's kid. He was quick-witted, endearingly cynical, and downright hilarious. He had a pale complexion that showcased his deep brown freckles and sported a classic side-spike haircut, complemented by a healthy amount of thick styling gel for added staying power. He was older by one year, and that one-year edge put him in the position of influence over me as we navigated our boyhood adventures together. Jimmy was more like Huck Finn, and I was more like Tom Sawyer, although we both contributed to the overall mischief. I've been told that I first met Jimmy when I was two, and since we both spent inordinate amounts of time at church, we spent most of our childhood together. We rose through the ranks of all the available children's ministry options shoulder to shoulder. Sunday school, kids' choir, Royal Rangers, youth group . . . we did it all, and we laughed through most of it.

When we were boys, Northwest acquired an elementary school directly adjacent to our A-frame church building. There was a large field between the two properties, with a tree line marking the boundary where the properties met. In total, the two buildings were approximately 300 yards apart. After the church purchased it, it was decided that its best use was to house the Sunday school and youth classes. When the weather permitted, it was a common occurrence to walk the 300 yards to Sunday school from the A-frame together. We'd saunter into whatever classroom to which we were assigned and find our seats. It takes a special kind of person to teach a children's Sunday school class and a supernatural act of grace to compel someone to volunteer for it. Not all Sunday school teachers are cut from the same cloth, though. We experienced a wide variety of temperaments and personalities—everything from gracious, gray-haired church ladies to militant, drill sergeant disciplinarians. When we were confronted with the latter, the mischief in us tended to poke its head out more than usual.

I remember one Sunday morning when Jimmy and I had apparently exceeded the limit of our teacher's patience. Heaven forbid that kids should laugh in Sunday school. The teacher slammed his fist down on the eight-foot folding table where we sat. He looked at Jimmy with a grave stare and pointed his finger at the door. Jimmy got up from his seat and followed directions. As he walked through the door, he looked back at me and grinned. I did my best to suppress my laughter. The teacher slowly made his way to the front of the classroom. In dramatic fashion, he turned to face the class, his eyes full of intensity. After a long pause, he said, "Would anyone care to join him?" I thought about it for a second. Then, after weighing all the options in front of me, I stood up and walked out the same door Jimmy had seconds before. By the time I reached the field between the Sunday school and the A-frame church, Jimmy had already hit the tree line at the midpoint. "Hey!" I shouted and waved my hand. As he spun, I saw that same sheepish grin amidst his freckles. I sprinted to catch up to him. We laughed as we made the long walk back.

Jimmy and I knew that church like the back of our young hands. We knew where and when the donuts would show up on Sunday morning. We knew the location of every office candy dish and what each would most likely contain. We were fixtures at the place. If we looked at the actual number of hours spent on the property, though, Jimmy would have me beat. His dad often had meetings after service on Wednesday and Sunday nights, which kept him there for hours into the evening. Wednesday night and Sunday were school nights. School nights meant homework needed to be done. As a result, Jimmy would often find himself alone and in the quiet, sitting on the floor in the hallway outside his dad's office, crisscross applesauce with his math book perched open in front of him. He often struggled to keep his eyes open after a long day at church.

He knew the eerie silence unique to an empty church building. It was part of being a pastor's kid.

This is exactly where he found himself on the evening of Wednesday, September 20, 1989. Twelve-year-old Jimmy Nichols was sprawled out on the thin, burnt-orange carpet of the hallway that ran between his dad's office and the doors of the A-frame sanctuary, staring at his homework in the fluorescent light as he waited for his dad. He was alone in that eeriness when it happened.

His freckled nose caught wind of an odd scent. He had long known the unique smells of that place, an eclectic bouquet of Lysol and cheap oil-based cologne from the parishioners. This one did not belong. After a curious sniff or two, he was able to place it. With a surge of adrenaline, he lifted his nose from the crease of his math book. His eyes, now wide open, followed. He was confronted with the sight of a steady stream of gray smoke seeping through the cracks at the tops of the doors to the A-frame sanctuary. The light from the rectangular, fluorescent fixtures that lined the ceiling of the hallway was being diffused like high beams on a foggy day.

Besides Jimmy himself, God only knows what thoughts rushed through his young mind. Maybe all the flannel-graph Sunday school lessons of the temple being filled with the Shekinah Glory moved up to the front of his brain. After all, we were Pentecostals. Maybe he thought, *This is it*! as the Spirit prompted his mind with all our boyhood shenanigans. Getting kicked out of Sunday school, stealing donuts from the church kitchen, and poking fun at the colorful characters who sat in the pews. Maybe deep conviction set in. Visions of the final judgment, the sheep and the goats. Maybe he thought, *I am a boy of unclean lips!* We had heard a lot about smoke and fire in God's sanctuary. We'd heard a lot about hell and brimstone, too. After all, this was a "Spirit-filled" church, and he was a bona fide son of an ordained Assemblies of God pastor.

Whatever went through his mind, Jimmy drummed up the courage to pick himself up off the floor and approach the double door to the sanctuary. He checked the temperature of the door with a quick press of his palm. Cool enough to proceed, he cautiously pushed it open. As he poked his head through, he saw something he would never forget. The front of the sanctuary was engulfed in flames. The fire popped and snapped like firecrackers in a frying pan as the heat hit his face. He noticed the blaze spreading from the right side of the platform up the choir loft toward the back wall, where the fake stained glass was located. The orange upholstery of the choir chairs was feeding the flames. What struck him most was the fact that the flames were moving aggressively toward the seam where the brick walls on the side of the sanctuary met the lacquered wood of the giant A-frame. His eyes shot up the wood paneling as it rose forty feet to the apex. He pieced it all together. It was as if the structure itself was a giant, brilliantly built campfire, complete with upholstered kindling and doused in lacquer gasoline. It was only a matter of time before the fire made the jump. His heart raced as he spun around and sprinted down the hallway to interrupt his dad's meeting. He burst through the door of the boardroom and shouted, "Dad! Dad! The church is on fire!"

PART 1

THE ORGAN

You must know that there is nothing higher and stronger and more wholesome and good for life in the future than some good memory, especially a memory of childhood, of home. People talk to you a great deal about your education, but some good, sacred memory, preserved from childhood, is perhaps the best education. If a man carries many such memories with him into life, he is safe to the end of his days, and if one has only one good memory left in one's heart, even that may sometime be the means of saving us.

Fyodor Dostoevsky

CHAPTER 1

If you have a pulse and are over the age of thirteen, chances are you've wrestled with existential questions that are somehow wrapped up in your relationship with your dad. I check all those boxes and am currently thirty-two years on the north side of thirteen. I'm knee deep in all things midlife, which makes me a prime candidate for existential questions. I have my fair share.

These days, part of my job is working alongside my Pastor, a thoroughbred man named Joby Martin. We both serve the church family that God is building in Jacksonville, Florida, called The Church of Eleven22. It's a special place. Joby is one of the best gospel preachers I have ever known. (More to come on him later.) When I say I work alongside Joby, I mean that in the most literal sense. Every week at just the right time, when Joby is turning the corner toward the close of his sermon, I get up from my seat and climb the side stage steps toward the keyboard that sits just to his right. After I push all the right buttons and turn all the right knobs, I place my hands on the keys in front of me and start to create. Honestly, I don't think very much about what my hands are doing. Whatever comes out finds its way from my heart directly to my fingers. I play, and I pray. Without fail, when I look down at my hands, the first thing that comes to mind is my dad. I come by the spot behind the keys of a piano honestly, and most of that has to do with him.

It seems cliché to say that my father was larger than life, but there is a level of objective fact to the statement. Steven Charles Olson stood 6'4" tall and weighed somewhere in the vicinity of 250 lbs., as I remember him. His Sunday suits and ties had to be purchased at Manny's Big and Tall, the local men's shop on the main street of the Chicago suburb where I was raised. The automatic seat of the family car, a white Lincoln Continental, had to be pushed to its rearmost position to accommodate the length of his legs. I know this because my seat was directly behind him. From time to time, he would grow a gruff beard, which would accentuate his Viking-like appearance. He was a true Chicagoan with that classic city accent that has a way of misshaping every vowel in the English language in the most endearing of ways. (Think Chris Farley with a fake mustache, sunglasses, and a Bears hat . . . you won't be that far off)

Dad loved everything about the city where we lived. It had a unique class and energy. It also had pizza. He was a local pizza connoisseur, well-versed in pies of every depth of crust. His love for it allowed him to maintain his fighting weight. He was a classic Chicago big guy. Once on a Florida family vacation, my dad was spotted by a local wearing a Chicago Bears t-shirt. The man approached us and asked if my dad played on the offensive line, as the Bears were playing the Dolphins the following week in the newly built Joe Robbie Stadium. We shook our heads but acknowledged the man's reason for asking. To a child of any stature, he was an imposing figure. To me, he was a giant. But there was another dimension to him that made him seem larger than life.

Although he looked like an offensive lineman, my dad was an artist, an architect by trade, and the organist at Northwest Assembly of God, where I spent most of my childhood. My dad made beautiful things. He designed beautiful homes for families to live in, and he made beautiful music for folks to worship God. He owned and operated his own small architectural firm in downtown Elmhurst on the west side of Chicago. I grew up looking at blueprints of mansions that came out of his beautiful mind. He designed homes for some of the most affluent folks in the city, and he was routinely recognized and awarded by his peers for his work. He was a genius at the drafting table. His sense of space and dimension was highly sought after. But he showed his heart on the organ bench. The deepest parts of him would find their way through all four of his limbs at once. Both hands and both feet were perfectly synchronized, creating a bed of chordal harmony that could melt the hardest heart. It was his prayer language. Intensely personal, yet commonly experienced by the inhabitants of our home and the community of faith to which we belonged. He played from a depth of heart and mind that is uncommon to most. Yes, he was a big man in stature, but what made my dad larger than life to me was the size of his soul.

He designed the home in which we were raised on St. Charles Road in Elmhurst, Illinois. The Olsons consisted of my parents, my older brother, my younger sister, and me. I remember it being built the summer before I entered the first grade. He had spent the first five years of my childhood wasting hours of the day in traffic commuting on Chicago freeways to his office. The combination of the stress of the commute and the sheer amount of pizza consumed pushed his blood pressure to an unhealthy place. He decided to move our family closer to the location of his office to shorten his commute and medicate his blood pressure rather than give up ordering pizza. So, he and my mom decided to purchase an open lot closer to his office.

My dad leveraged his connections and expertise to build our new home for a reasonable price. It was a great place in a great neighborhood with mature Elm trees whose branches came together to create a canopy over the streets. St. Charles Road was busier and wider than most of the roads in Elmhurst. I could walk to the end of our driveway toward the steady flow of traffic, turn toward Lake Michigan, and see the top half of what used to be called the Sears Tower downtown in the distance. The house was big enough for my siblings and me to each have our own bedroom. There was a beautiful kitchen with custom oak cabinets and a matching table for family meals. There was also a living room with vaulted ceilings and skylights, which allowed natural light to filter in as it passed through the Elm trees above. The back yard was sizable for a suburban home.

Without a doubt, the liveliest room in the house was the front room downstairs with windows that looked out over St. Charles Road. It was crammed with musical instruments of various kinds. My first set of drums, a shiny black Yamaha baby grand piano, my brother's bass guitar and amp, a few early model keyboards, and the granddaddy of them all—my dad's three manual Allen Organ, complete with pedal system and enough speakers to make the joists of the house tremble. It had more buttons and levers than the cockpit of a 747. But when Dad sat on the bench, he made playing it look effortless. He could manipulate the tones to his desired effect with virtually no work at all.

We played a lot of different music in that room, from Andrae Crouch to Bruce Hornsby and the Range. My brother would bounce between bass and piano, while my dad bounced between piano and organ, exchanging looks and laughs along the way. As I got older, I would try my hand at each to keep up. I learned by being thrown into the deep and cutting my teeth early. Drums came fairly easy to me for some reason. I had a natural knack for tempo and groove. I also developed a deep love for the grand piano. I loved the way the sound resonated through the house. Yet, I could never work up the nerve to sit in front of all those intimidating buttons on the organ. It was in a league of its own, and Dad was the only one qualified to handle it. The organ bench was where he was most at home.

Of all the music that was made in that room, the most meaningful happened late in the evening hours. My brother, sister, and I would be tucked into our respective beds. My dad would sit alone in the front room of the house and begin to open his heart. He found another gear as he swayed back and forth on the bench, his shoes set to the side so he could feel the pedals with his toes. I could hear him talking to God through the music from my upstairs bedroom. I'd stay awake for as long as my eyelids would allow. Eventually, they would give up, and I would fall asleep to the vibration of the wall next to the bed.

Yes, my dad designed and built houses for a living, but he also built temples—grand palaces of worship through the sounds he made downstairs. And yes, I was raised in the house that he designed on the outskirts of Chicago. It was built out of two-by-fours and sheet rock. Yet in a weightier and more sublime sense, I was raised in the nightly temples that he built at the organ bench. As I lay upstairs, I felt like the young boy Samuel, making himself comfortable enough to sleep next to the Ark of God's presence. To this day, these have been some of the most influential moments of my life, and they began in my dad's heart.

Other than my house, I spent most of my time at the church where we attended. In fact, there were weeks when it could be argued that we spent more time there as a family than at home. Northwest Assembly of God was located on the corner of Wolf and Kensington in Mt. Prospect, Illinois. It took us roughly thirty minutes to get there from our house on the Chicago toll roads. Our weekly rhythm began with the drive to church early on Sunday morning, as Mom and Dad were responsible for preparing the music. There were two services on Sunday morning. After they were over, we would drive back for lunch and a few hours of rest. At about four o'clock in the afternoon, we would drag ourselves back into the family car and head back for Sunday night service.

During the week, there were Wednesday nights with Royal Rangers and Missionettes for the young boys and girls, while the adults were in big church. These were a sort of spin-off of Boy Scouts and Girl Scouts for young Pentecostal kids, complete with uniforms to wear and badges to earn. I progressed through the various age-based stages throughout my childhood. Straight Arrows for the youngsters, Buckaroos for elementary age, and Pioneers for the angsty teenagers, each with their own distinct wardrobe and award system. It admittedly got less appealing the older I got.

Thursday night was choir practice. Our whole family attended. Friday night was youth group for my older brother. It was back and forth—north and south—every week. We knew every pothole on the route. There were two forty-cent tolls to be paid each way. Twenty cents short of a dollar for a one-way trip. I remember my dad pulling up to the toll booths to pay the fare. They looked like the starting gates at the Kentucky Derby with little white plastic baskets that collected the coins. Paying tolls became so routine for my dad that he could grab the required coins from the ashtray without looking and fire them in the basket with pinpoint accuracy without stopping. We were back and forth so much that I'm certain our family is responsible for footing the bill for most of the Chicago freeway system. I still look for a commemorative plaque when I'm in the city.

You might think that all the time spent at church and the frequent trips on those toll roads would lead to a sense of menial drudgery. I mean, what could a little kid find appealing about spending that much time in church? Images of little boys bound up in tight collars and neckties, wearing uncomfortable shoes and having overly slicked-back hair, forced to sit still for extended periods, probably come to mind. I'm sure some kids grew up that way. Not me. That would be the farthest thing from my experience. To me, church was magical. To this day, I can't recall a time when I went begrudgingly. There was so much to love about it. I loved all the nooks and crannies where I could hide. In the dead of the deep Chicago winters, I used to tuck myself behind the long, heavy trench coats that hung on the racks in the lobby. From that spot, I was a spectator to what I am convinced was one of the most eccentric and colorful collections of humanity that has ever gathered in one place.

CHAPTER 2

Northwest Assembly was Pentecostal and charismatic, which meant that it attracted a particular kind of person. I don't mean in terms of age, socioeconomic position, marriage status, or race. On the contrary, they came in every shape, size, and color. I mean a certain kind of person in terms of general excitement and expectation for what would happen next. Specifically, what God would do next. They were not a cold, stoic group of people. On any given Sunday morning, Sunday evening, or Wednesday night, there was a palpable sense of anticipation that lingered in that place.

There were older folks like Bob and Evie Evenson, both so tall that they had to duck their heads like giraffes when they walked in the front doors. Big Bob (as I called him) would have his giant leather Bible cover tucked under the arm of one of his bold, plaid-patterned sport coats. His white patent leather dress shoes seemed like they were a mile long. His wife, Evie, had the unique ability to maintain a sense of genteel elegance while touting a trombone. Her long, floral dresses and matching heels were somehow enhanced by carrying the long, jet-black trombone case. It was the most uncommon of accessories.

Big Bob would regularly exercise the spiritual gift of speaking in tongues during the time of corporate singing. As the music would die down, Bob would gear up like a foghorn, uttering the most oddly beautiful collection of vowels and consonants you could imagine from the back row. Toward the end of his utterance, he would begin to run out of breath. His face would turn a deep shade of red as he strained. We would all hope that he would make it to the end of the sentence, which was a challenge considering we couldn't understand what he was saying. Often, someone else would pipe up with an interpretation, as per the apostle Paul's direction to the church in Corinth. At other times, we all just sat in the quiet and waited to see what would happen next. Bob and Evie were passionate about the Spirit of God, and their demeanor showed it. I don't recall ever seeing either of them without a giant smile on their faces. Their love for God was contagious.

There was Angie Alexander. She was like an aunt to me. Tall and elegant with a beautiful black complexion. She was a single career woman with a sharp mind, and Northwest was her family. She invested in it faithfully over the years with time, talent, and treasure. She had a beautiful singing voice and would often find herself behind a microphone. When Angie would sing, there was always a deep sense of maternal compassion and care that would materialize in the room. As she used her gift, that part of God's character would rise to the surface.

Pat Popover. Yup, that was her name. Pat was an older single woman with a very white complexion who wore large, ornate rose-colored eyeglasses. She had one of the most comprehensive collections of silk neck scarves I've ever seen. I don't remember seeing her without one tied delicately around her neck, regardless of the season of the year. Come to think of it, I don't recall ever seeing her wear the same one twice. As a young boy, I began to develop the morbid idea that if I left the safety of the coat racks to sneak behind her and untie whatever scarf she happened to be wearing, her head would roll down her shoulders and tumble to the ground. I was too scared to try it. One Sunday night, Pat got up and gave a testimony, thanking God for providing her with a brand-new car. My memory is hazy on the make and model, but I remember the shiny, white pearl finish of the paint. She proceeded to tell everyone that she would henceforth refer to the car as "the silver cloud of glory," and she did.

Jim and Bob Osters were two brothers in their mid-thirties with families of their own. Bob and Jim played drums and bass in the church band along with my dad. It was a family affair. There's something beautiful about brothers on drums and bass. You can feel the family in the groove. It was in their shared blood. I soaked up their every move like a sponge. Jim used his personal drum set at the church and was very protective of it. It was a seven-piece Ludwig, and I couldn't keep my hands off it. He would always hide a pair of drumsticks somewhere in the sanctuary in the event he forgot his stick bag. Over the years, I developed a sonar-like ability to locate them. He would often walk into the sanctuary to find me behind his drums and become visibly agitated at the sight, but it was never enough to stop me from doing it.

There was also a group of folks who were more colorful than the rest. For example, Steve Held was a middle-aged single man. He had some social quirks that would pop to the surface from time to time. He would sit in the row directly behind the youth group and, mid-sermon, remove his shoe, peel off his sock, and trim his toenails, one foot at a time. The sound of the clippers would make the teenagers squirm in their seats. Oddly enough, Steve also had a brilliant mind for American history and was energized at the opportunity to share his passion in conversation. He had a slow, low delivery in his speech as he unpacked little-known facts about the Founding Fathers.

Then there was Ralph and Eva Lerner. I can't comment with any level of certainty on their actual ages. They could have been thirty-eight years old as easily as they could have been eighty-five. Ralph used a walker to get around. It had pockets around its perimeter for his Bible and other necessary supplies, which included his clarinet. It would have been impossible for him to be mobile without the walker. He would wield it forward with a loud clunk and drag his feet behind. His speaking voice was high-pitched and terse and could be heard anywhere on the property. Ralph had the most intricate pair of spectacles I've ever seen. They were multilayered, three lenses deep, in various degrees of potency. His wife, Eva, was short and stout and of German descent. She had large, rosy cheeks that would deepen in color in the colder months. She would accompany Ralph as he scooted along with his walker, wearing long floral dresses whose hemline would allow her footwear to be seen. Black combat boots. This was the faith family of my childhood. A colorful cast of characters with odd quirks and genuine hearts.

The church building itself was as quirky as the congregation. The giant A-frame structure had been built in the late 1950s. It had orange brick walls and a steeply pitched roof that was covered with dark black shingles. A tall metal cross stood in front of the building, extending up to and beyond the apex of the A-frame roof. It towered over the road. Inside, there was a fireside room, a fellowship hall, a kitchen with bright yellow cabinets, and a choir room that was referred to as "the pit." The pit was built in the shape of a baseball diamond. It consisted of four levels, each successively dropping two feet as they got closer to home plate or where the choir director would stand. The tenors and basses would sit in the upper rows (left, center, and right field), and the altos and sopranos filled the infield. When the room wasn't in use, it was a perfect place for a young boy to work out pent-up energy, jumping up and down the levels. The jumping may have even happened a time or two *during* choir practice, but you'd have to ask Jimmy Nichols about that. I would never think of it.

The sanctuary, which sat under the giant A-frame, could seat around 900 people in pews upholstered with a dark teal fabric. My mom would often comment that on the night of November 2nd, 1978, I was nearly born in one of those church pews. Apparently, Mom and Dad cut it close. The color of the pews matched wonderfully with the burnt orange carpet that clad the floors. It was a modern interior designer's worst nightmare. There were eight-foot orange brick walls on each side with dark-stained glass window insets. Not the ornate kind you would see in the Gothic cathedrals of Europe. These were big blocks of bold color. Red, yellow, blue, green, orange, and more orange. After Sunday night services in the winter months, I would press my nose against the cold glass and squint my eyes to see the streetlights on Wolf Road refract through the color. My breath would steam up the glass, diffusing the beams.

The walls eventually gave way to rich, brown lacquered wood paneling that covered the interior of the A-frame. The highest point shot up thirty or forty feet from the top of the orange brick below. As a child, the ceiling seemed high enough to be mistaken for the gates of heaven. Classic octagonal pendant chandeliers hung down from the panels, creating small, focused beams of light on the pews below. On the back wall of the sanctuary was the sound booth, which Dick Johnston manned faithfully every week. It was commonly acknowledged that Dick was deaf as a stone, but he was eager and consistent, and he could talk a good game. Our services were routinely interrupted by feedback blaring through the PA system due to his lack of skill. Whenever it would happen, most of the heads in the place would turn toward Dick with a glare. On a few occasions when the feedback persisted longer than usual, Dick would throw up his hands like a prisoner of war and shout,

"I don't know!" Things always seemed to work themselves out, allowing the service to continue, and it never bothered him enough to stop showing up.

Towering thirty feet or so above the sound booth on the back wall was a small square opening that looked out over the sanctuary below. On the other side of that opening was a small room known as "Will's Nest." Will was the guy who manned the spotlight during the annual church Christmas and Easter Musicals. The only way to get up there was to open the pull-down staircase in the ceiling of the hallway in the church office upstairs. Once you climbed that staircase, you were in the bare framing of the roof. There were a few more crude wooden ladders and landings to scale before you eventually hit the platform where Will did his magic. On your final approach to the platform, you were greeted by a small, wooden custom-made sign bearing the words "Will's Nest" branded into the wood. It looked like it belonged in an old west saloon. Will's giant spotlight took up most of the room on the platform. It had color-coded levers on the side of it that could be pulled to change the color of the spotlight for the desired theatrical effect—deep red for the passion scenes of Easter and light blue for the starlight over the Bethlehem manger.

The pulpit was at the front and center of the sanctuary. Initially, it was built of ornately cut wood and was engraved with a Scripture reference that I can't recall. It was large and imposing and could easily sustain the pounding fist of the preacher who stood behind it. Somewhere along the way, someone decided to replace it with a smaller one, built of clear plexiglass, allowing parishioners to see the preaching pastor's taste in trousers every week. There was always some dear saint who was trying to keep it clear of dust and fingerprints before services. It never worked. The choir loft sat directly between the pulpit and directly in front of another block of stained glass that stretched up to the apex of the roof. On Sunday mornings, the sunlight would bring the blocks of glass to life, casting a rainbow of primary colors onto the choir members below. It illuminated the plexiglass pulpit, making it look like the crystals in Superman's fortress of solitude.

The choir loft is where one could regularly see (and hear) my mom, Vicky. She loved being in the choir. Her rich alto voice became a staple in the overall sound that it produced over the years. It was deep and emotive, with a wide vibrato that has grown in depth as time has passed. She doesn't sing as much these days as she did in years past, but it's not for a lack of desire. My mom was full of life. This was most evident in the context of the Northwest Assembly of God choir. She was, and still is, one of the purest examples of a people-person that I've ever known. Her deep sense of compassion and empathy for—well, for anyone—was (and still is) always at the forefront of her mind and heart. Often, it came at great personal cost. It could be experienced equally in her natural desire to walk alongside people who were in dark seasons of emotional duress, as well as in her tendency to break out in boisterous laughter at the drop of a hat.

My mom's laugh was a force to be reckoned with. The word *cackle* would apply. At church, it was her calling card and would quickly become the focal point of any room she was in, be it the pit during Thursday night rehearsals or the Sanctuary on Sundays. She would often force the preacher's hand into acknowledging her laughter from the pulpit during the sermon. It could not go unaddressed. Should a joke sneak into the content of the sermon, her laugh would ping-pong through the A-Frame. "Thanks, Vicky," the preacher would say. Everyone sitting in the pews knew the laugh's source and would smile in response. Everyone but me, that is. I would be lying if I said that I wasn't embarrassed by it, even at a young age. At the time, I couldn't even tell you why.

At this point in the story, I was unaware of my mom's history. As time has passed, I have learned about events in her childhood that were formative in shaping who she is today. Namely what made her so quick to empathize with others. Her dad, Luke James, left before she was born to fight in World War II. He came back a different man. Part of his dealing with the trauma of the war was distancing himself from those closest to him, including my mom. She didn't meet him until she was eighteen.

Mom's childhood consisted of living just above the poverty line in the rural Midwest and being bounced around between the homes of extended family and members of the church. It could have shut her down, but I later learned that the laughs that echoed through the A-frame were equal parts defiant joy and coping mechanism. In hindsight, I understand that my mom's sense of resilience in the face of her past was nothing short of miraculous. She was a broken person, choosing to put one foot in front of the other in faith. We are all a product of the formative experiences of our past, whether joy or pain. My mom is no different, including God's supernatural act of grace to use life's deepest depths and highest heights to shape our character into his desired outcome. That is what makes the Jesus lover unique. His constant attention to all things toward the ultimate purpose of His glory and our good.

To this day, one of my mom's proudest personal achievements, aside from raising her kids, was directing that choir. Her passion for God and song beamed out of her as she waved her arms in time, making intense eye contact with the folks in front of her. They could see the moisture start to build up in the corner of her eyes as her heart leaked up to her face. It didn't take long for it to get there. They would respond with adoration of God in loud choral harmony. It was beautiful to listen to and moving to behold. As I write this, my mom is in her late seventies, and she still refers to her years of involvement in the Northwest Assembly of God choir as some of the most meaningful of her life.

This is why church was so exciting to me as a kid, and these were some of the most formative memories of my early childhood. More than the colorful characters, it was seeing my mom and dad serve together at church. They were in tandem. Complimentary. While she was up with the choir, my dad was swaying on the organ bench just off the platform in accompaniment. The stuff I soaked up from my dad at the organ in the front room of our house informed what he did at church, and vice versa. It was all the same. Shoes off, set to the side of the bench as he created. The organ itself was virtually the same. Three manuals, a pedal system, and hundreds of buttons to push. Church and home, home and church, making church feel like home. I saw their passion and dedication for seeing God worshiped in corporate song under that A-frame roof. They were alive in God's presence with God's people in God's house. It all made something come alive in me. I developed a deep sensitivity to what would happen when people came together to worship God. It happened earlier than I could fully comprehend or put into words.

I can recall sitting in a children's choir rehearsal in the basement of Northwest as a young boy surrounded by my closest childhood friends. We couldn't have been much older than four or five at the time. I was holding a folded piece of sheet music with the simple melody we were being taught notated in oversized quarter and half notes hanging on a treble clef. I can't remember the name of the song or the way the melody developed, but I'll never be able to forget what transpired in my gut that day. It was as if God reached down from his throne in heaven and put His hand on my stomach. There was a collision in me. The tenderness of my boyhood heart ran full force into the weight of Glory. It was a Bethel moment, like when the heavens were opened over Jacob.

God was there, and it shook me to the core. I began to weep in the small plastic chair I sat in, flanked by my peers. At first, I tried to hide the tears by shielding my face with the sheet music. Eventually, the sense of God's presence took such a hold on me that it could no longer be hidden. My throat became tight as water poured down my face.

I didn't know what to do. So, I lied. I concocted a story that I cut my eye with the corner of the sheet music. Ashamed, I ran out of the room looking for a place to hide. I opened a door to a staircase in the back corner of the building that nobody ever used, likely installed to keep the building up to code. The stairwell was vacant, dark, and quiet. I crawled under the first flight of stairs, tucked myself into the dark corner, and wept for what felt like hours—with God.

I remember walking into the sanctuary after my Straight Arrows class had ended to find my parents. I knew where they would be, at the front of the church leading worship. Those services tended to linger on well into the later hours. It wasn't uncommon for me to find them there. As I entered, I saw a group of seventy-five to a hundred grown men and women holding hands in a circle around the circumference of the A-frame room. My dad was on the organ bench, swaying as he played. The Oster brothers were there next to him on bass and drums. The music they were playing was in a minor key, but it was upbeat. Jim was playing a quick two-beat rhythm. The pattern of the kick and snare drum sounded like someone chanting *um-pah, um-pah* repeatedly. Bob, his brother, bounced along on the bass guitar, providing the tonal foundation. My dad brought the harmonic shape of the music to life through his hands and feet. Even from a young age, I recognized the sound as having a distinctly Jewish feel. It was in a minor key, but it carried a sense of celebration, even victory.

As the music played, the people holding hands danced in simple, choreographed steps. Each held their neighbor's hands high in the air as their feet moved along with the rhythm. Their feet shuffled right and left and then crossed over in tandem. I stood there, watching in my red uniform vest. The joy on their faces was contagious as they made their way around the sanctuary. This was more than "Ring Around the Rosie." It was praise. It was an act of triumph. I stood there and took it all in. I was familiar with the story of the Israelites' deliverance from the hand of Pharaoh. I knew about Moses, God's appointed man. I had learned about the parting of the sea, about Pharaoh ordering his men to pursue the Israelites to the death. I also knew about the sea swallowing up the Egyptian army as Israel watched in safety on the other side.

> *I will sing to the Lord, for he has triumphed gloriously; the horse and his rider he has thrown into the sea. The Lord is my strength and my song, and he has become my salvation; this is my God, and I will praise him, my father's God, and I will exalt him. The Lord is a man of war; the Lord is his name.*
>
> (Exodus 15:1-3)

It all started to come together in my soul as I watched the people dance to the music my dad was creating. Somehow, I knew that we were involved in the same story. There, on the corner of Wolf and Kensington, thousands of years later, this eccentric community of people was celebrating in much the same way and for the same reasons. And I saw my dad playing his part. I'm sure my mom was one of the hand-holders that night, although I have no direct memory of seeing her. As I watched, I began to understand that this was what we, the Olsons, were about:

reveling in God's victorious presence. Leading people into an awareness of it. It instilled a sense of purpose and direction in me as a young boy. My dad's depth of soul and my mom's emotional genuineness were passed to me as an inheritance through experiences like this. It's tough to distinguish what's nature and what's nurture. It doesn't matter. It all pointed me in the same direction. That is, God was pointing me in the same direction. I was being marked by His indelible fingerprint. It was too deep to deny and too big to forget. In the Psalms, David described this sort of thing:

> *How lovely is your dwelling place, O Lord of hosts! My soul longs, yes, faints for the courts of the Lord; my heart and flesh sing for joy to the living God . . . For a day in your courts is better than a thousand elsewhere. I would rather be a doorkeeper in the house of my God than dwell in the tents of wickedness.* (Psalm 84:1-2, 10)

David talks about the presence of God being more desired than rich food, more valuable than pure gold. For some reason, I understood it. It resonated with me. What else besides God's sheer grace would pull the heart of a boy so close and lead him into this sort of awareness? I was too young to do anything to deserve it. I had no mind to develop a doctrinal construct for why this could even happen. I didn't need to; it just did. Like the undeserving thief who was promised paradise, God was drawing me close to His heart.

CHAPTER 3

Sanctuary is a beautiful word. It simultaneously conveys a sense of the sacred and the secure. The word *sanctuary* takes these two realities and makes them inseparable. In the sanctuary, one can be overwhelmed by the majesty and holiness of God, yet be completely vulnerable, exposing their truest nature. We all long for this. We were all made for this, for a place to live in reverent awe and be known on the deepest level all at once. The A-frame was the place where I reveled in God's presence as my dad played the organ on the right and my mom, robed in white, sang along from the choir loft. It's where I lost myself in the wonder under the shadow of their blessing. It's the place where the innocence of boyhood belongs. In the shelter sanctuary provides, boyhood can blossom in vibrancy, beauty, and power. Its fragrance can freely fill the air like holy incense.

But in the small hours of the morning on September 21, 1989, I felt a hand gently shake my shoulder. My mom had come to share the news. "Honey," she said. "Don't be afraid. The church is on fire. Daddy and I want to be there to see it." My mom had arranged for someone to come and stay with my siblings and me while she and my dad made the drive to see it happen. It seems odd to think about it now, but there was no question in either of their minds whether it was worth it or not to leave in the middle of the night to watch the church burn. That place was central to the heart of who they were and to who we were as a family.

I wasn't there to see who and how many assembled to pay their respects to the A-frame as the flames ate it up. But as I drifted back to sleep, images of a small band of the most committed parishioners huddled together in the amber glow of the blaze played on the back of my eyelids. I imagined my parents, Pastor Jim, Angie Alexander, Bob and Evie, Pat Popover, and the Osters brothers, all grieving as they watched. Jimmy was the only kid present in my dream. He stood in the middle of the group, a blanket draped around his shoulders, with an air of heroism from being the fire's initial discoverer.

The next morning, I didn't see my mom and dad. They had stayed at the church through the night. My siblings and I were woken up, fed, and taken to school by the babysitter. When I entered the classroom, my teacher greeted me with empathetic eyes. My mom had made her aware of what had happened. She knew how important the church was to our family. I remember working through the school day with an odd feeling in my gut. Something

I hadn't felt before. It felt like grief or loss, but I was too young to fully understand what it meant. I found it hard to focus on school, being preoccupied with the jolt that came from the news. I discovered that I shared the same desire as my parents. I wanted to see what had happened with my own eyes, and I wanted to talk to Jimmy about it.

That afternoon, my mom picked my sister and me up from school. The lack of sleep showed on her face. Dad had gone straight from the burning church to his office to begin the workday. We made the familiar trip up the 294, through the two toll gates to the corner of Wolf and Kensington. By that time, the fire department had done all they could, but the damage was severe. They had saved the wing of the church that housed the classrooms, the kitchen with the yellow cabinets, and the pit, which was filled with water from the fire hoses. But the sanctuary smoldered in a giant pile of smoky ash. The scent permeated the air. A few of the large arches that had supported the wooden A-frame jutted up into the sky, the tops burnt off. They looked like the fractured rib cage of a giant skeleton. The metal cross that towered over Wolf Road was still standing. It became a focal point of hope for everybody. Will's nest was no more, gobbled up in the blaze. The seven-piece Ludwig that belonged to Jim Osters, my hiding place behind the lobby coat racks, the octagonal chandeliers, the blocked stained glass—all of it had been burnt to the ground. The teal pews where I almost entered the world, my mom's choir loft, and my dad's organ. They had all been lost, too. I couldn't believe it. It left a hollowness in my stomach. As I stared at it, I noticed the burnt hymnal pages lilting back and forth in the breeze over the wreckage and the clear plexiglass podium that those dear saints had tried to keep free of fingerprints. It was now melted into a puddle at the front of the sanctuary.

I saw Jimmy. We acknowledged each other with a somber nod, unable to speak. I guess we didn't know what to say or how to say it. Our boyhood kept us from immediately accessing the vocabulary to process what had happened. In our youth, we hadn't yet experienced this kind of loss, not to this scale. We retreated to the small park that sat across the parking lot. It had a set of swings that faced the church property where we had spent a lot of time together.

We sauntered over and sat shoulder to shoulder in the swings and started to pump our legs back and forth as we took it all in. The words began to come. Jimmy described what had happened the night before. When he spoke, there was a foreign heaviness. It was so different from the laughter we shared during our boyhood antics. Occasionally, a small glimpse of his familiar cynical levity would break through, but it wouldn't last long. The lack of sleep and the weight of what we were looking at from the swings would overtake it. I didn't know how to process it either. There was an obvious sense of sadness that pervaded the sight of it. But there were moments in the days that followed where I would think about the fire and have an odd desire to burst out in laughter. The reality of what had happened was too big to be pigeonholed into a category, and even if it could be, I was too young to do it.

Chapter 3

The fire had a massive impact on the life and rhythms of our family. My parents knew that the church could by no means be relegated to a building. Even I knew that, as young as I was. The church wasn't the fake stained glass or the A-frame roof. What made Northwest was the people who sat in the pews, not the pews themselves. But walking in the fullness of that understanding was hard to come by in the immediate for all of us. Loss is loss, and this was real. I had traveled to the corner of Wolf and Kensington to worship God with my family since the day I was born. My mom and dad had invested decades of their lives in that church before I drew my first breath. Now, the A-frame that had reached the heavens had been diminished to a pile of ash and rubble. It felt as if somebody had taken a pickaxe and dislodged the cornerstone from the structure of our family rhythms.

The next few weeks were a flurry of activity, especially for my dad. In addition to his duties as a father of three, the owner of a small architectural firm on Chicago's West Side, and the church organist, my dad had been appointed to serve on the church board. It goes without saying that the fire led to an uptick in the workload on that front. There was information to be sorted through and communicated. There were decisions to be made, pivots to be considered, and questions to answer. There were ramifications on all fronts: insurance, logistics, legal, and financial. It all added to the complexity of dealing with the fallout. My dad found himself squarely in the middle of it all. He had a deep love for Northwest Assembly, and it weighed heavily on his 6'4" frame, pushing his blood pressure higher than usual. I would often catch him in the middle of heated conversations on our corded home phone after he came home from work with the pastors and other board members. He would pace back and forth in the kitchen while the curls stretched and recoiled along with him. Rebuilding the church was the preeminent topic of conversation at family dinners. Our time around the table would routinely feature an update on the day's happenings, direct from the board. I felt like I had a front seat to it all.

It wasn't long after the night of the fire that the church board had a meeting with the Mt. Prospect Fire Marshal. The Marshal was a classic Chicago civic servant, fully decked out in blue. He wore shiny black boots and had a shiny silver badge pinned to his chest pocket. A bushy mustache accentuated his gruff demeanor. As a kid, I had always felt that fire and policemen brought a certain air with them when they were around. Especially the ones from Chicago, but it was all I knew. They were there for public safety, but they had a way of simultaneously evoking a sense of danger. We called them *cops*. They drove classic boxy Chevrolet squad cars with loud sirens and had holstered handguns. They had thick accents. These are the guys they make TV shows about—and this was the Marshal. He fit the mold to a T. It was the Marshal's duty to run a full-fledged investigation on what transpired at the corner of Wolf and Kensington on the evening of September 20th, 1989. He and his team would sift through the evidence, compile the data, run the forensics, and build an accurate narrative. No stone would be left unturned. For as young as I was, I could tell that he took his job very seriously.

Chapter 3

The reason I can speak so knowledgeably about what the Marshal looked like is that I started to see him more frequently as time went on. He showed up at the house on more than a few occasions with a clipboard, gruff demeanor, and mustache in tow. When he came, he and my dad would usually disappear behind closed doors for official business. At first, I didn't think much about it. After all, my dad was on the board and had an obvious interest in the outcome of the investigation. It made sense that he and the Marshal would feel the need to engage in private conversations. But the regularity of his presence increased, as did my curiosity about what they were talking about. So, I opened an investigation of my own. I wondered if the Marshal was over at Jimmy's house as much as mine. I asked; he wasn't. I would insert strategically vague questions into conversations over dinner in an attempt to string together a storyline. When the phone rang, I tried to place myself within earshot of the conversation. I even pressed an ear up to a closed door from time to time.

As it turned out, the Marshal was at our house for good reason. He had combed through the data. He had built a narrative. He had corroborated the experts' findings, and with a high degree of confidence, he had reached a conclusion about how the fire started. All evidence pointed to the organ that sat to the right of the platform.

On the evening of September 20th, 1989, Steven C. Olson had neglected to turn it off after the Wednesday night prayer service. As a result, an electrical short occurred in its internal wiring. That short created a spark. That spark turned into a small flame. That flame grew to not only consume the organ itself, but the entire sanctuary in which it sat. It jumped from the organ on the right side of the platform to the upholstered chairs in the choir loft where my mom sat. From there, it continued to spread until it ate the lacquered wood paneling that lined the ceiling of the A-frame. The Fire Marshal discovered that Dad had torched the place, and he had done it with the instrument that he wielded so beautifully as the eclectic congregation that made up Northwest gathered to worship. As the results of my own personal investigation became clear, I was flooded with intrigue and emotion. It hit me like the end of one of those cheesy crime scene investigation shows. *No!* I thought. *It can't be.*

As my investigation continued, I realized that my dad was the elder appointed to accept the check issued by the insurance company to cover the damages. It was no small sum. To complicate things further, the church had decided to move forward with my dad as the architect who would design the new building. It all converged in my young mind. Steven C. Olson, the deep-souled organist/architect who sat across from me at the dinner table every night, was the prime suspect in a serious arson investigation, and the Marshal was duty-bound to leave nothing wanting in trying to establish a motive for foul play. Dad was in the crosshairs of the Chicago Blue, and the entire church family that we called our own was party to it.

I weighed the scenarios for a few days. Could it be possible that my suit-and-tie-wearing, white Lincoln Continental–driving, dinner-praying, swaying-playing father was involved in a money-making scheme that cost the church its sense of sanctuary? The formality of the Fire Marshal's demeanor made me wonder. At no point in any of the interactions with him that I was party to did he ever break a smile. There was no joviality to be had. He was no Barney Fife. He was more Tommy Lee Jones in *The Fugitive.* The slightest notion that my dad had an alternate insidious identity made my skin crawl. It was oddly disorienting. I wanted to believe that I knew my dad. He was by no means a perfect man, far from it. But an arsonist? I couldn't make the jump to that conclusion. I made up my mind that he was clean.

Sure enough, the investigation lasted a few weeks, and through all the questioning and probing, the marshal was never able to construct a cohesive argument sufficient to make a legitimate accusation. When all was said and done, he officially cleared my dad of any suspected wrongdoing. As far as the law was concerned, Dad was off the hook. The fact that the fire that destroyed Northwest Assembly started in the organ never made the headlines of *The Chicago Tribune*, but everyone close to the story knew. It created an awkward tension in our world. Church functions, dinner parties, church band rehearsals: they all carried the residue of what had happened and how he was involved in it. My dad de-escalated the situation with humor. When the topic came up in conversation around the house or the church, he would often shout, "You can't prove anything!" He'd storm out of the room with his index finger pointed straight in the air. You knew he was operating in jest, but he left you with the sliver of the thought that he was hiding something.

Northwest would spend the next year and a half meeting in the gymnasium of the middle school down the road while the debris was cleared and the new building was designed and constructed. A town hall-style meeting was held in the old fellowship hall, which had survived the fire, to discuss the new sanctuary. My dad sat up at the front of the room with the pastors as people filed up to the microphone to give their opinions on how it should be built. The meeting was marked by a palpable tension between two differing opinions. There was a contingent of folks who wanted to rebuild the sanctuary as it was. They wanted the building to retain the sense of reverence that existed in their nostalgia for what it had been. As they spoke, I understood what they were talking about. After all, much of my boyhood experiences with the beauty of God's presence had occurred in that place. I didn't want to let go of any of that. The other side of the argument was championed by the forward-thinkers. They saw the trajectory of church culture changing, and they wanted a building to accommodate it. They were more function over form. More basketball hoops and fewer chandeliers. This was the camp my dad was in. I sat in the meeting and watched him haggle over the emerging trends in church design. The more traditional folks didn't like the idea of the sanctuary feeling like a community center. I knew my dad knew his stuff and I trusted him, but there was a part of me that had a hard time letting go of what had been. The old A-frame represented all things safe and sacred to me.

When the debate was over and the votes were cast, it was decided that the sanctuary would be a large multipurpose room. Way more modern and functional than the old A-frame. It was designed by Steven C. Olson, Ltd., a small architectural firm on the west side of Chicago, much to the Marshal's chagrin. It took approximately eight months to build the building. My family and I would drive by the construction site on the way to the middle school gymnasium, where we set up for church every week. As we did, my dad would point out the progress, "Looks like they've got the steel." On the few occasions the whole family accompanied him to the site midweek, I would go to the park across the parking lot while my dad walked the grounds with a white hard hat. He would engage in conversation with the tradesmen, pointing out details here and there with his fingers. I could tell he took pride in his work.

The first Sunday we met in the new building, the ushers greeted people at the new double doors and handed each a colorful church bulletin. Its cover featured the new church logo. A classic Holy Spirit dove design with a slight alteration. The dove's tail morphed into the shape of a flame. The caption underneath read: "Northwest Assembly: Refined by His fire, aflame with His love." It was on the nose and slightly cheesy, but it was a fitting bookend for the experience.

Things eventually came full circle. The traditionalists came around. Big Bob and Evie Evenson would duck through the doors to the new sanctuary. He, with his white patent leather shoes, and she, with her giant trombone case. Steve Heald repositioned himself behind the youth group on Sunday nights and continued to cut his toenails during service. Dick Johnston continued his career as an under-qualified church soundman from the newly elevated sound booth in the back of the building. Jim Osters got a shiny new set of Gretsch drums to replace the ones he lost in the fire, and I kept stealing his sticks. My mom and her choir mates received brand-new white choir robes with reversible stoles: royal blue on one side and crimson red on the other. They wore them as they stood in the new choir loft that sat behind the pulpit. My dad even paid homage to the old stained glass from the A-frame. The new window hovered over Mom's choir loft, spilling a prism of sunlight just as it had before. In a pinnacle of irony, Dad even got a brand-new organ. It was perched up on the right side of the platform, where it had been before.

Meeting in the new sanctuary brought a sense of completion to things. That heaviness that had sat on Jimmy and me as we pumped our legs back and forth faded into the background. As the church worshiped in the new space, a fresh sense of the sacred began to develop in me as well. It took some getting used to, and it wouldn't ever be the same. But God's house, at least the brick-and-mortar part, had been rebuilt and was filled with the sound of His people singing, preaching, and praying again.

CHAPTER 4

Sometimes the things we experience in the immediate and material can point us to a deeper sense of meaning. It doesn't happen often or right away. It usually takes a minute for the plot to develop, for the story to unfold. But every once in a while, we are struck with a sense of perspective. There is a convergence of the twists and turns of our lives with a broader sense of purpose and design. I'm not talking about resolution. In fact, the perspective can be paralyzing. When this happens, it's not uncommon for us to find ourselves on our knees, crying out for a light on the path through the exile of grief and fear.

Sometimes that light comes the way we envision it, sometimes it seems like it doesn't come at all. It's sobering. It's challenging. In any and every case, we are not the same on the other side of it. In the years that followed the fire, I began to notice some changes in my mom and dad.

Nothing was said to clarify why the shift was occurring. It was all very vague. Nebulous. To me, it felt like a dark, slow-moving shadow overtaking our home, covering everything with a heavy sadness. The weekly rhythms didn't change. In many senses, it was business as usual. My dad was still busy at work designing award-winning homes for Chicagoland's elite. My brother, sister, and I went to school. The family piled into the white Lincoln Continental for Wednesday night church, Thursday night choir practice, and Sunday morning and evening services, just as we always had. Mom still stood in the choir loft, and Dad still took his shoes off at the organ every weekend.

But the air in which it happened began to change. Something had slithered into the garden of our home. Somebody was deceived and took a bite of some forbidden fruit. The dinner table became quiet and stoic. A palpable tension began to materialize in the way we interacted as a family while we sat together. It moved from the top down. Strike the shepherd, and the sheep will scatter. My dad became less inclined to engage in conversational updates on matters of the church board and more tuned in to the glow of the TV in the adjacent living room. Seemingly, he did it because it required less work. My siblings and I, confused, followed suit in a reactionary state of despondency. We all shared a common desire to leave our seats as soon as possible to do other things that were more enjoyable.

As I entered my junior high years, my mom, once full of life, drifted off into a deep pit of depression. She did her best to keep up with her responsibilities. She ironed Dad's shirts and made peanut butter and jelly sandwiches for my siblings and me. Looking back, I am astonished at her ability to keep herself afloat. But there was a hollowness in the way she attended to it all. I didn't recognize it. For me, it was a foreign country, a desert.

Likewise, I could sense my dad moving into a state of passive retreat. He was starting to disappear. After work and the silence of the dinner table, he would move in one of two directions. One was a swivel chair in front of the living room TV. With the Keebler cookie tin that my mom kept stocked with Oreos in his lap, he would lose himself in a dopamine rush of high-fructose corn syrup, local news, and Chicago sports until he dragged himself up to bed. He looked and lived as if he were enslaved to something. An invisible enemy that no one could see. Neither he nor my mom would relinquish the details. For reasons of personal shame or our preservation, they were silent. We were east of Eden, ousted from the place of flourishing.

I said there were two places my dad would gravitate toward. I am grateful for the second. It was the organ bench in the front room. From time to time, my dad would still make his way to the front of the house. When he did, we knew not to follow him. He needed to be alone. He would flick the switch that turned the organ on, bringing it to life with a soft hum. He removed his shoes, just like Moses did at the burning bush, and he sat and swayed as he played and prayed. I recognized the songs. Many of them were the same ones he always played, but somehow the music felt different. I could sense the mourning in it.

If you pick up a Bible and thumb through the Psalms and pay attention to the words that are there, you'll be surprised at what you'll find. It's not the plastic religious jargon that so many suppose the Bible to be. It's the real stuff—gut-level honesty. You will find ecstatic elation and celebration. You'll discover joyful triumph and the expression of deep gratitude for unearned blessings. But if you keep at it, you'll understand that walking with God can lead you into some other territory as well. You might end up in the shadowlands. There are those kinds of prayers, too. You'll find words of accusation. Death wishes for enemies and their children. Doubt. Anger. You'll find songs sung in isolation and deep desperation. That's what these were. I could hear it in the music that poured from his heart through his fingers and toes. I didn't know why, but I knew my dad was in pain. And I heard him wrestle with God over the particulars in the music that he played.

As I've grown up, I've learned that God doesn't owe me answers. I used to think that He did. I never wanted to admit it, but I used to believe that the world revolved around me. I lived like God had an obligation to me to make things make sense, and I used to think that He needed to fulfill this obligation on my timetable. I could even bend Bible verses in my own mind to justify my frame of thought. I could make the letters on the pages jump through hoops like a circus animal for my own entertainment. It turns out I didn't know God. I knew who I wanted Him to be. Ironically, that looked a lot like me. It must have been some shift for Copernicus to discover that the Earth wasn't the center of the universe. The rock that his feet were planted on actually revolved around something else. A revelation like that can change a man.

Here's a mystery: God's nearness to me as a young boy . . . the times I spent worshiping God with his people in his house, with my mom and dad, the dancing and singing, the moment I spent with Him underneath the stairs in tears . . . It was all very real. It was pure and genuine. In those moments, God was larger to me than life itself. I learned so much about who He was and who He *is*. But as formative as those experiences were, they were incomplete. It's hard to understand, but God loved me too much to allow me to continue in my ignorance. It wouldn't be just or loving of Him to allow me to continue to believe that He was in my debt. He owes no man an explanation. He never has, and He never will. He used pain and loss to teach me a lesson. At times, I thought Him unkind. Even as I write this, I'm still growing in my understanding of what He was, and is, accomplishing in it. "Oh, the depth of the riches and wisdom and knowledge of God! How unsearchable are his judgments and how inscrutable his ways!" (Romans 11:33).

I prayed for my parents. I wanted so badly for whatever was lost to be regained. I didn't even know what that was, but I knew it was gone. As time went on, they continued to allow their deep personal separation from one another to grow. They simultaneously maintained face at Northwest. Even as a young teenager, the duplicitous nature of it was exhausting for me to observe. In a sense, I knew they were doing the right thing by remaining faithful to God's house with their time, talent, and treasure. And I knew there was something altruistic and right about them continuing to bring my brother, sister, and me there. Even so, I could sense something deeply flawed in the way they were going about it. The heart was gone. I can only imagine how tired they must have been from carrying the load. No one can do that sort of thing for a long time; it's unsustainable.

Things began to erode. My dad's God-given depth of soul became a breeding ground for harboring ill will. The same gifted mind that created mansions in which the affluent would raise their families became fixated on concocting collections of bitter words. It was destroying our home. The same strong emotional current that created harmony at the organ bench was being hijacked to generate the opposite. The tide was shifting, and the waves were growing. Love and order were reverting to chaos. We were all lost in it.

My dad was a beautiful instrument steeped in complexity. More nuanced than the organ on the right with all its buttons and knobs. Just as he could generate beauty through the keys in front of him, so the Spirit of God could manifest himself through my dad's beautiful soul. He was designed to resonate with that Spirit and meant to channel love, joy, peace, patience, kindness, goodness, faithfulness, gentleness, and self-control. Much like the organ that was left on in the A-frame the evening of September 20, 1989, something shorted out in him. That short turned into a flame. A brutal enemy fanned that flame into a fire, and that fire raged into a blazing inferno that burned our house down.

My dad's aloofness and despondency started to morph into anger toward my mom and us. There were regular fits of rage, almost as if some sinister force crept inside his fragile heart and took it over. His mind, his hands, his tongue . . . created to be instruments of righteousness became tools of wrath. With deep cuts in his inner man, he backed into a corner like a mortally wounded animal. The anger came out with accusations of ingratitude toward my brother, sister, and me. We waded through piles of guilt for our entitlement to who he was and what he did for us. It was new and disorienting, leaving me confused, yet knowing that there was a part of him that was right. I didn't understand the resentment that he was harboring. I couldn't comprehend how much he continued to provide a home for our family in the midst of it. But when the heart of the father becomes hostile and turns in on itself, the child has no choice but to feel that his world is upside down. What I had once known as benevolent and gracious had become defensive, even inimical.

That kind of anger can ruin a man. And it did. Over the following years, he began to erode. He sought a way out and began to construct an alternate reality for himself. Dealing with the pain of real life came with too much resistance. It was easier to start believing that there was another way. Some place, some people that wouldn't cost as much. A greener pasture. My brother moved out. After my senior year of high school, I left home for Bible College in the Twin Cities. Ironically, I ended up doing much the same thing my dad did, and I never looked back. Home was too volatile, and there was too much adventure and self-discovery to be had looking through the windshield to pay attention to the rearview mirror. While my mom and dad coexisted back home, I got my degree. My little sister would eventually attend the same school that I went to, three years behind me.

Two weeks after my sister graduated from college, a moving truck arrived at the family home that my father had designed on St. Charles Road. It was largely unannounced. My dad closed the storefront of his small architectural firm, loaded up the truck, and moved to Southern California to pursue the reality that he had been quietly constructing for himself, unbeknownst to any of us. My mom was left alone, fighting the demons of depression. Our family home was a shell of its former self.

I need to say something about my dad. When I think about it now, my heart swells up and my eyes get watery. It's something I didn't realize until much later, and it adds to the complexity of this story and of his character. I demonized him for years. I needed a villain. I needed someone and some way to help me make sense of the destruction. A scapegoat to pin it on. He was the obvious target. This is what inequity, the fracture of an intimate relationship, does. It creates a brutal awareness of what I feel I'm *owed* or what I didn't get. As odd as it is, this is where my dad's accusations of my entitlement and lack of gratitude ring true. What I've since discovered is that my tendency to villainize my dad is born of the same stuff as his creating an alternate reality. It's the path of least resistance. It's settling for convenience because it's there. The truth is, we're all reeling from the loss of Eden, sitting staring at the smoldering sanctuary. We're all living in the wake of distrust. Everyone. Nobody wins. The debt is real. It must be paid for, and no one can afford it. My mom couldn't, my dad couldn't. Nor can I.

Here's what moves me. My dad waited to leave until my little sister graduated. This is not coincidental. Although he spent more than a decade building his fictitious, preferred reality, he didn't act on it until he had done what he felt was necessary to take care of his kids. I don't think it was a matter of duty or obligation. In his own way and in his own pain, he was operating out of love. My sister and I both graduated from Bible college with no debt. He wanted to see that we were taken care of. Somewhere in the middle of his inner turmoil, there was a subtle but deep paternal affection. The residual evidence of God's gracious heart. But a wound is a wound, and although it's taken me some time, I've discovered that a father wound is one of the worst kinds. For years, I didn't even know I had it. I was oblivious to myself as I pushed forward, distracting myself with success, achievement, and momentum. Men do that and it never works.

There is a place in the heart of a boy that only a father has access to. It's the place where adventure and wonder are born. The power of a father's affirming presence in that place gives a boy the courage to explore the unknown, to discover himself in the presence of God, and to live with curiosity about what could be. For me, that place was where the music was, where my father was. It was the front room and the sanctuary. When my father drifted away in emotional despondency throughout my formative years, he unknowingly passed his wound on to me. The sanctuary he had raised me in burned to the ground, and the music that filled it left. I had to try to write my own earlier than I was ready to.

GUIDED REFLECTION

Eden must have been a glorious place. The absolute power and purity of God's imagination fleshed out in untainted creativity around every corner. Everything from the most grandiose natural wonders (think the giant Redwoods of Muir Woods, or the expansive vividness and color of southwestern desert sunsets) to the most miniscule and seemingly insignificant (picture the intentional path of the common Carpenter Ant, or a singular hidden blossom at the highest branch of middle eastern Almond Tree) all in complete alignment with the intention of the Author. But, as I imagine it, even its natural beauty would pale in comparison to the seamless bond of love and trust that existed between God and the man and woman whom He held to be the pinnacle of His creation. They were like branches grafted into the great "vine" (John 15:5). Second to that would be the seamless bond of love and trust that existed between the man and woman under God's blessing. Think of it: no guilt, no shame, no hiding. There was no occasion for any of them. Only a pure, unadulterated bond of safety and intimacy in God's presence. Relationship in its purest form. They were one even as Jesus and His Father were one (John 17:22).

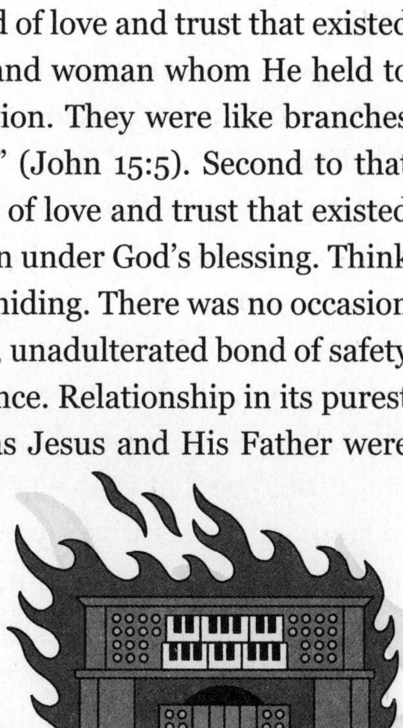

Juxtapose this reality with what it must have been like for Adam to find himself facing eastward as he walked away from the beauty of that garden with an angel wielding a flaming sword at his back. Instead of Adam's feet touching the lush beauty and intentionality of Eden's soil, the very ground beneath him now pronounces dusty curses at him with every step. He is confronted with the new and foreign reality of feeling isolated from both his closest earthly companion and his Maker. His mind is now clouded with the guilt and shame that are born as a consequence of the serpent's deceptiveness. Where there was once a steady and immovable confidence that undergirded his every thought, there are now seeds of resentment and revenge from the imbalance in which he finds himself. But far worse than the turmoil of his mind is the wound he carries in his heart. He lost his home, and along with it his childhood innocence. It burned to the ground. The music went away. Everything that once was can no longer be, and there's nothing he can do under his own power to bring it back.

Okay, let's talk about you. I've shared a part of my story, and we've just spent some time wrapping our imagination around Adam's. What about yours? The shift of focus may come as an unwelcome jolt to the system. But if you've read this far, you may have developed some curiosity that might propel you forward, however frightening that might be. It could be that you've never allowed yourself the time to stop and assess where you are and how you got there, let alone *who you are* and how you got to be that way. If so, you're not alone. Many of us have decided that we don't have time to consider our wounded hearts. The thought of dealing with it is too daunting and too expensive. And in the end, what does it really matter?

Paying attention to who we were, who we are, and how we got to be that way seems ultimately unhelpful, without any real practical value for the present. It is better to find ourselves trudging eastward, avoiding our wound along with Adam, in an attempt to pull greener pastures out of the cursed ground. At least we can measure the progress and use it to try to justify our existence to the rest of the world. We may even have begun to build our sense of identity and value on what we've achieved while sweating over our labor. It's how we cope. This can look like the trophies and plaques on our shelves, numbers in our bank accounts, and shiny cars in our garages. They've become welcome distractions from rediscovering who we were really created to be. We've demonized the innocence of our childhood and forgotten how to play in God's Garden. We haven't heard the music for a long time and have grown accustomed to the silence. As a result, we believe our worth is purely found in the practicalities of what we can produce. We think of ourselves as soulless machines. But in the end, we find that our hearts have formed lifeless callouses pushing us increasingly in the direction of becoming less human, and God's reflected image in us loses its clarity.

If what we're discussing is putting a lump in your throat and something strange is beginning to leak from your eyes, blurring the words on the page, let me capitalize on the moment and admonish you with some real God *truth*. You weren't designed to live life that way, and there is nothing weak about acknowledging your wound. In fact, in God's redemptive process, the courage and honesty that come with facing who you actually are become the gateway for real and genuine restoration. It's not the end, it's the beginning. In Jesus talk, it sounds like this: "Blessed are the poor in spirit, for theirs is the kingdom of heaven" (Matthew 5:3). Or as my pastor Joby Martin says, "If you wanna be free, you gotta be honest."

Your sense of sanctuary and safety may have burned to the ground, leaving you isolated and alone. Your earthly mother or father may have started the fire and left you to deal with the fallout by yourself. A serpent may have slithered into your garden and unleashed hell. As a result, you may be well down the eastward road with nothing but silence and your wounded heart as your closest friends. If you're honest, you're living out of half of your heart while the other half is dark and dormant. You've decided that trying to grin and bear it until the end is the only viable course of action.

If any of this is true, you're not alone. It may seem completely illogical in the moment, like you're at the end of yourself, but you're actually at a starting line. Before we move on, I'd love to invite you to pause with me and open yourself up to the reality that there's an Author to your story and His intentions for you are good. He's intimately acquainted with each twist and turn that got you where you are. He knows about your wound, how you got it, and how long you've been carrying it. It is a part of His story, too. He was betrayed by those closest to Him. At best, they were asleep in the heat of the crucial hour, leaving Him in isolation, and at worst . . . a kiss that led to a cross. He embodied David's prayer in Psalm 22 as He confronted

His pain and asked God an honest question: "My God, my God, why have you forsaken me?" (Matthew 27:46).

You should know it's not how His story ends. Jesus confronted the pain instead of ignoring it. Hebrews mysteriously tells us that Jesus's earthly suffering played a role in making Him *perfect*. The scars from those wounds would ultimately play a crucial role in opening the eyes of one of His doubting deserters. They are still at work today. Because of His story, your wounds don't have to be how your story ends either. For now, the best thing to do is acknowledge who you are, including the most painful parts, to yourself and to Him. You can invite all of who He is into your story. He'll do the rest.

PRAYER

Father,

I'm slowing down enough to realize that there is a real wound in my heart.

Some things have happened to me that have forced me into a heartless kind of living. Fear of my wound has been shrinking my reality.

I've been ignoring dealing with it because I'm afraid of where it might take me, and what it might mean.

I'm starting to see that my efforts to ignore my wound and move ahead in my own strength aren't working. It's not getting better. I need healing.

Thank you, Jesus, for showing me how to be present with my woundedness and see it as part of a grander story.

I entrust myself to You.

In Your power and authority, I pray.

Amen.

PART 2

THE GIBSON

Friendship is something that raised us almost above humanity. This love, free from instinct, free from all duties but those which love has freely assumed, almost wholly free from jealousy, and free without qualification from the need to be needed, is eminently spiritual. It is the sort of love one can imagine between angels.

C.S. Lewis

CHAPTER 5

It's been said that the blessing is in the breaking. To that, I respond, . . . "You have no idea!"

My best friend, Ben, was the first person who laid eyes on it, *it* being the 1969 Gibson J45 mentioned in the title of this section of the book. The guitar had seen some life and had the wear and tear to prove it. It had a sizable gash on its face, the sunburst finish had a well-worn patina, and the neck had been broken and repaired. But it all seemed to add to the overall vibe. It was beautifully distressed. The kind of distressed that people try to manufacture by strategically sanding furniture or cutting holes in the knees of jeans. But this was the real thing. It was the best kind of honest. When you wore it, it made you feel like you were experiencing everything that it had. It was fantastic.

At the time, Ben and I were traveling with a well-known Contemporary Christian Music (CCM) artist as supporting musicians. Ben was one of the best electric players around (and still is), and I was somehow succeeding at convincing people that I could play drums for a living. We were scheduled to play a show at the Frank Erwin Arena on the campus of the University of Texas in Austin that weekend. There was a slight mix-up in the dates, which allowed Ben some free time to roam around the city before the rest of the band showed up. And, as I've learned, Austin is a great place to find high-quality used guitars. Ben walked into a guitar shop on the south side of Austin and saw it hanging on the wall. He was kind enough to pass me the tip on it. Truth be told, he passed on buying it himself because he already owned a few vintage Gibsons, and he was having a hard time justifying purchasing another. A guy has to know his limits. I capitalized on his conscience.

Upon my arrival, I promptly rented a car, drove to the shop, plugged the guitar in, and threw down the money to make it my own. It was worth every penny and then some. It took no time for the guitar to make a name for itself in our small community of musicians, which caused a little bit of friendly tension between Ben and me. He would say he should have bought it. I would smile as I formed chords on the well-seasoned rosewood fretboard. At that point, we had already shared enough life to weather that sort of thing. But there's no way we could have known what challenges would lie ahead.

Ben and I were like brothers, like Jonathan and David. Ten years before he introduced me to the guitar, we met under what now seems to be providential circumstances. I was a freshman at North Central Bible College in Minneapolis, Minnesota, and was traveling with a choral group of around forty people. The group would roam around the Midwest by bus, doing concerts in cheap tuxedos and long, unflattering black dresses, recruiting prospective students along the way.

One of the most adventurous aspects of these trips was staying in host homes at the churches where we would hold the concerts. It was a roll of the dice because you never knew where you would end up or who you would meet. I remember the bus pulling into Kalamazoo, Michigan, on a Saturday night and my choir mates filing into the sanctuary of Ben's home church. I noticed the pews and carpet. They were a matching shade of emerald green. It brought back memories of the terrible color clashes under the old A-frame. Later, Ben and I would refer to that place as the "Emerald City."

Ben was a senior at the small Christian high school run by the church. To his parents and teachers, he had seemingly unlimited raw talent and potential, but his heart was set on spending it all on a post-graduation run with a pop-punk band called Nobody's Heroes. (You can't make this stuff up.) What I didn't know at the time was that Ben's high school music teacher was a distant relative of the chair of my school's music department. They were Italian and knew how to get stuff done, like the mafia. They had conspired together to place me in Ben's home in hopes that I could sway him into shunning his rock 'n roll dreams for enrollment in Bible school the following fall. A gutsy move. The guy with the housing list yelled "Olson" and pointed me in his direction. So, it began.

That first night, Ben and I hit it off. The term "fast friends" would apply beautifully. We stayed up well into the night trading stories about growing up in the Pentecostal church, about what college was like . . . and about *music*. We both loved it. Specifically, the kind of music that moved the heart toward God. We discovered that we shared an affinity, a language we both spoke, and a passion that burned deep within us. As we talked, the time flew by, as it often does when you're having fun. The conversation was natural and easy, and the level of youthful enthusiasm was high. When we couldn't stay awake any longer, we both retired. The next morning, I crawled out of bed, tired from the lack of sleep, donned my fifty-dollar tuxedo, and headed back to join the rest of the choir at "Emerald City." We led worship and performed our usual repertoire as a part of the Sunday morning service. When it was over, we both found each other and talked about how much fun we had the night before. I waved goodbye as I boarded the bus, not knowing if or when Ben and I would see each other again.

Ben showed up as a freshman the following fall. I was ecstatic to see him. The mafia conspiracy had worked. The music department and I were the better for it. We became classic college buddies at North Central Bible College. For the next four years or so, we experienced life together, learning about who we were and who God was. We played a lot of music, and we developed a close friendship as a result. There was a substantial amount of laughter, some dating heartbreak, and many shared moments in what I would describe as a *heavy* sense of God's glorious presence in worship and prayer.

One weekend, we found ourselves playing music at a funeral celebrating the life of a missionary named Cal Olson, who was a graduate of North Central. Cal had spent most of his life trying to reach the people of Bangladesh with the good news of Jesus. He had died of old age. During his ministry, he saw very few converts. He lived with constant threats from the people he was called to serve. He was mocked and beaten on several occasions. It was sobering to hear people talk about it. This was apostle Paul-type stuff. There was a reverence in the way people remembered Cal.

After the funeral, Ben and I huddled in the back of the church and reflected on what we had experienced. We vowed to each other then and there that we would never spend the life and energy that God had given us on meaningless endeavors. To this day, we haven't. That kind of stuff makes people's hearts connect. It's rooted in something bigger than you. It's rooted in God.

After Ben and I graduated from college, we both stood up in each other's weddings. I first met his wife, Jen, in my freshman orientation group at Bible School. She's a saint. I watched them fall in love. Ben was there the night I met my wife, Ashley. We both knew she was completely out of my league. He talked to her more that night than I did. (The only thing that kept that on the up and up in my mind was the fact that he was already engaged to Jen, and she was definitely meant for him.) We loved spending time together as young married couples, enjoying things that young couples do without the responsibility of children. There were late nights, spontaneous fast-food runs, and a lot of light-hearted silliness, or as Ben's wise father, The Pops, would say, "Fully Unadulterated Nonsense (F.U.N.)." The Lord led us both into a season of involvement in the business of music-making. Ben was a guitar player and producer, and I was a recording artist and drummer. Our gifts were complementary, and we would work together as much as possible. I ended up signing a record deal in 2004, which moved Ashley and me to Nashville. It was hard for us to consider living in different places, but Ben and Jen decided to stay in the Twin Cities, where we had gone to Bible School. We put major pressure on them to follow, but it didn't take. I should also mention that Ben had been highly committed to leading worship at a local church plant in the suburbs of St. Paul throughout the entirety of our college years. The tiring kind that involved weekly setup and teardown. He served faithfully there for a long time. He didn't want to leave. He was that kind of guy.

Through an odd twist of the Lord's sovereign sense of humor, I was offered the chance to travel with one of my childhood heroes, Michael W. Smith, as a touring drummer about a year after moving to Nashville. I still can't quite wrap my head around how it all happened, mainly because when I was asked to play, I hadn't had a pair of drumsticks in my hand for about five years. But you don't turn this kind of opportunity down for small reasons like that. I still remember standing on our back porch while taking his call. "Are you interested?" He asked. "Are you crazy?" I asked in return. He took the chance on me.

For the next six years, I juggled my fledgling artist career with traveling with Michael. It was an exciting season. I would throw a guitar in the back of my red Volkswagen and drive myself to some small rural church in the southeast to play a singer/songwriter night for thirty folks. Upon completion, I would head back home only to jump on a private jet to play drums in an arena in a major city the next night. I'm sure my Volkswagen got better gas mileage. It was awesome. I got to travel the world sitting behind one of the most influential musicians I have ever known and see him use his God given gift to lead people in worship—night after night. And I got paid for it. Like, it was my job.

But I missed Ben. Fortunately, he had begun to make a name for himself as an electric guitar sideman. Michael knew who he was. I leveraged every bit of influence I had with my new boss to land him the same opportunity that had been afforded to me, knowing that, if it happened, it would mean we would continue to share major life experiences together. It worked, and we did. For three years, we were on team Smitty. Ben never officially moved to Nashville, but we would rendezvous on the weekends during touring season in cities like Austin. That was the next best thing. (By the way, if anybody asks, I am deeply indebted to Michael for giving me or . . . for giving us . . . those kinds of experiences. They were a gift. Love you, brother.)

Enter the Gibson. This leads us to that fateful day when *the* guitar and I became acquainted. Ben found it; I bought it, and the case that held it. I placed it gingerly in a spare bunk on the bus, played the show at the Frank Erwin

Center, and headed home that night. It was the greatest guitar I had ever held in my hands. Certain guitars define what a guitar should sound like. You hear it and you think, *I've heard that sound a thousand times . . . and loved every one of them.* This was one of those. The tone wasn't too bright; the sound wasn't too big. When plugged in, it fit an in-ear monitor mix perfectly, panned right up the middle. But it sounded like magic to the naked ear all by itself. Who knows how many songs had already come out of it, but I knew for a fact there was more to come. I was going to pull them out of it. The guitar was transcendent, and I loved it.

By that time, my wife and I had welcomed our son, Brody, into the world. Similarly, Ben and Jen had welcomed their first daughter, Anna. Although we lived in different cities, we would cherish the times when we could see each other's kids with our own eyes. Couples who bring babies into the world tend to retain close ties with other couples who have done the same thing at the same time. There were a lot of firsts to talk about and a steep learning curve to weather.

Ben and I were both on the road a good bit during that season. He more than I due to the opportunities that were opened by his highly sought-after skill set. When we were together, I noticed our conversations starting to shift. They were less Peter Pan and more slow and steady. Less about going for the green and more about grabbing the nine iron and laying up. We were growing up. Having kids will do that to you. Don't get me wrong, we both loved traveling. There wasn't much not to love about it. The rush that came with making the sounds we got to make, seeing people by the thousands move toward God as a result, and the catering. There was a tremendous upside. But as the days passed, we grew to love other things more.

Somewhere in this season, we both went on an unusually long international tour with Michael. Five weeks in Canada, South Africa, and Brazil. In one trip, I saw both coasts of Canada traveling by bus, the very southernmost tip of Africa (not by bus), and experienced an unstoppable barrage of red meat from a legit Portuguese-speaking Gaucho. It was exhausting, yet amazing. But upon my return home, something strange happened. When I walked in the front door, jet-lagged with a suitcase in hand, Brody looked at me like a stranger. He was hesitant to run to me. It was the first time I had ever experienced something like that, and it hurt. It got my wheels spinning.

Simultaneously, I was offered a job as a worship leader at a big church in Phoenix called Christ's Church of the Valley, more commonly known as CCV. I can honestly say that up to that point, Ashley and I had never entertained the idea of moving to the desert. But I had known for a while that God was leading me toward serving in a local church setting. My son's hesitation when I walked through the door made this particular prospect all the more appealing to us. So, we thought about it and prayed. We even went to Phoenix to check it out. Ashley cried. We didn't want to leave Nashville, but we knew that we wanted to set ourselves up to be great parents over the next ten years or so. That rightly seemed the weightier priority.

It was no surprise to us that Ben and Jen were having similar conversations, parallel to ours. Jen's patience with Ben's absence grew thin, especially with Anna in the mix. He was putting her sainthood to the test. Jen and Ashley would confide in each other about that kind of stuff. I would hear about it when she deemed it appropriate, but it didn't surprise me when I did. Then, an intriguing thing happened. The leadership at CCV approached me about hiring someone else, along with me, to help carry the load. They sent me a few references. Mostly Nashville-based folks, of whom I was faintly familiar. But I'd be lying if I said my heart didn't immediately leap at the prospect of Ben moving his family to the desert with us to start a new chapter of the story. It was a long shot, but worth the chance. I took on the role of the conspirator. I made the introduction, set up the meeting, and waited to see what would happen, knowing that the church staff would be out of their minds not to hire him on the spot immediately.

In the months that followed, Ashley and I weighed the decision to relocate with the new twist of Ben and Jen being possible companions on the journey. Their presence would definitely sweeten the deal and minimize the unfamiliarity. We chewed on it constantly. They were doing the same thing simultaneously in Minnesota. The decision-making process felt a little like an eighth-grade dance. We were waiting to see who would make the first move. There were many conversations of "Whatcha thinkin'?", or "You know what would be great . . .," and "Maybe our kids will get married?" Crazier things had happened. We hemmed and hawed for months, knowing that the decision to be made was a big one. As it played out, Ashley and I were the first to commit. Ben and Jen would follow a few short months later. A wise lyricist once penned the phrase "Go west, young man." We both knew that phrase well. So, we did.

CHAPTER 6

The week of the Olson move was a blitzkrieg of sorts. I played my last show with Michael W. and Amy Grant in Lancaster, Pennsylvania, on Sunday evening and went to sleep on the bus. Ben had opted out of that tour for another opportunity. He was missed, but Stu G from the band Delirious? took his spot. He could hold his own. Monday morning, I woke up in Nashville, got off the bus, and headed home to start packing. Our moving company showed up on Tuesday. We signed the sale of our Nashville house on Wednesday. Thursday morning, my father-in-law and I made a left-hand turn on I-40 with the bare essentials (the Gibson in tow). My family would follow by plane. By Sunday morning, I was sitting in the church where I would spend the next five and a half years of my ministry career. We signed the purchase agreement for our new home in the far northwest corner of Phoenix proper on Monday.

What a difference a week can make. One Monday, I was a Nashville-based touring drummer; the next, I was a desert-dwelling suburbanite. We chose to live in one of those small, master-planned, walkable communities that you find out West. The ones with the over-the-top amenities, low HOA fees, and fancy euphoric-sounding names like *Vistancia*. It had a ring to it. When I walked into the community center to get my picture taken for our family's pool pass, I noticed a sign overhead that said, "Welcome to a more balanced way of living." I couldn't help but chuckle.

When Ben arrived, we dove into the work with full force. It was what people call a *megachurch,* but it fell on the north side of that category, with weekly attendance measured in the tens of thousands. It was large, influential, and on the cusp of a massive generational leadership transition. The physical campus was impressive. It was laid out over eighty-five acres like a private college with a slight theme park twist. The main worship center was complete, featuring a Starbucks in the lobby and a full-service café. There was a pizza shop run by a true-blue Sicilian named Sal. It was called Papa Don's, a tasteful spoof honoring the founding pastor.

There was an energetic culture about the place. People loved being there and were generally excited to be a part of the largeness of it. The worship ministry had been understaffed for its growth (thus our being brought in). There was much work to do. We both knew that a strong, vibrant worship culture would help the church through the changes ahead, so we didn't waste any time getting our hands dirty.

Chapter 6

There is no way to overstate the culture shock we were both experiencing. We went from tour buses and catering to staff meetings and HR emails. It was a bizarre shift, but we were spending more time with our wives and babies. It was the first time our family had legit benefits. I actually went to the dentist. That was a big deal. Just weeks before, I was meandering around the hidden hallways of large theaters and arenas with event-specific backstage passes draped around my neck. I wore them with pride, a literal badge of honor. I collected them. In stark contrast, it's amazing how I developed an aversion when I was asked to wear my staff badge around the church campus. Even though it had my picture on it, I felt like a character in the Pink Floyd video, "The Wall." I've never been a natural joiner, and this situation didn't hide it. Ben and I, and our families, were together in the same city. We hadn't experienced that since Minneapolis. We could drive to each other's homes for dinner. We would order takeout and eat outside in the dry evening air, trying to put language to what was happening while our kids played in the pool. It was difficult to do. It felt like whiplash. We got to lead worship together on a routine basis, which felt like home. Ben would lead from one of his many electric guitars, and I would lead from the Gibson. I bought a bunch of those guitar humidifiers to compensate for the extreme climate, but I figured if the guitar were going to shift, it probably would have done so already. After all, it was ten years older than I was.

What happened over the next five years is difficult to encapsulate in words. As I write this, I am five years into the next phase of my life (a decade from the move to Phoenix), and my pulse still quickens as I look back. It changed me. To a certain extent, we all know that life has peaks and valleys. Seasons of oasis and seasons of desert. It's very rarely cut and dry, and black and white. At least not for long. My experience is that the older I get, the more complex it becomes. I'm secretly hoping that there is a wise old sage phase one day out there when it gets easier, but I'm not holding my breath.

I used to think that I could avoid pain by making wise decisions. I used to think that the point of living was to try and make it through the game with the least number of nicks and scratches as possible. I've come to realize that a measure of pain is inevitably part of the process. The crazy thing is, it's all *grace*. A life void of pain lacks character and nuance. It lacks flavor. By way of analogy, when that guitar left the factory in 1969, it was brand spankin' new. Every aspect of it had been inspected, and boxes had been checked to prove that it was ready to live out in the real world. But it was not yet what it would eventually become, and much of that would come as a result of the bruises, scrapes, and burns it would pick up along the way, in the case of this analogy, a broken neck.

There's a track record for this sort of thing. Jacob wrestled with God and limped away with a broken hip and a new name. Joseph fell from the heights of his father's affection to the depths of his brothers' betrayal. After years of tumult and turmoil, he reached a point where he was graced with the perspective of God's ultimate plan. There must have been a beautiful release in his spirit when he said, "As for you, you meant evil against me, but God meant it for good. . ." (Genesis 50:20). Paul had his thorn. Moses had his stutter. David had his Absalom-heartbreak, and Jesus had His cross. All of these were a means to an end for God's ultimate purpose to be fully realized. There is an inherent beauty in brokenness as it is seen as the backdrop for redemption. But it takes a minute to figure it all out. It doesn't happen all at once.

The first two years of the Phoenix season were about getting settled into the new normal. Ashley and I were figuring out how to be a married couple without me leaving every spring and fall on a tour bus. I'm sure Ben and Jen were experiencing the same thing. There was a richness in it. Family dinners, preschool drop-offs, and weekend excursions to Laguna Beach to avoid the oppressive heat. Those things were the fruit of the decision to leave Nashville. We knew it was a good move.

On the church front, Ben and I began the process of building a healthy and sustainable worship ministry. The pace of growth at CCV put us in a position to move forward and backward simultaneously, improving on decisions made in the past while forging ahead to meet the demands of the future. It was tricky work. There was a decent amount of necessary conflict that comes along with progress. The tussle of trust building that leads to decisions made, money spent, and culture built. It wasn't as simple as making music, which was what we had been doing. It took a hefty amount of relational and emotional intelligence to balance it all. Ben was a master at it. We worked like an octopus, eight arms and one brain. The years we spent together paid off in our ability to anticipate what the other would do and make complementary moves with little communication. This was true on both the musical side and the people side. One was a beautiful analogy for the other. I remember getting the chance to see Tom Petty and the Heartbreakers in San Diego before Tom passed away. It was the opening night of the Hypnotic Eye tour. As it all went down that night, I was floored by what my eyes and ears took in. It was the fruit of decades spent creating and performing together. No computers, no click tracks, no tricks— just instruments (a *lot* of amazing guitars), time, and experience. "How good and pleasant it is when brothers dwell in unity" (Psalm 133:1). They were in a well-worn groove. I felt a little like that with Ben.

A couple of years in, I remember the guy who hired us pulling me aside, requesting a meeting. I didn't think much of it at the time, as it wasn't an uncommon occurrence. We decided on a time and place. When the meeting rolled around, I walked into a small office on the second floor of the worship center to see what he wanted to talk about. He began to lay out the organizational pressures that the team was experiencing as a result of quick growth from his perspective. I nodded my head while trying to understand what he was talking about. Until I moved to Phoenix and took the job, I could count the years I had spent working in a large organization on zero fingers. Writing songs—yup. Leading God's people in worship—for sure. I even faked my way through playing drums with Michael W. for six years. But navigating the complexity of organizational growth—*nada*. It was a brave new world, and I was a rookie. The more he talked, the more he began to sound like the teacher in the old Charlie Brown cartoons. I nodded my head and pretended to listen. When he had finished his explanation, he paused. Then he asked me a question. I heard it loud and clear. Thinking back on it makes me wince. "How would you feel about Ben moving into a leadership position over the team?"

The question produced a funny feeling in my stomach. It was unfamiliar and strangely foreign. It felt a little bit like taking a bite out of a forbidden fruit. Up until that point, Ben and I had lived life shoulder to shoulder. We were brothers in arms, sharing foxhole time. Separate (at times debatable) but equal. Historically, I had been his biggest fan. I wanted him to win, especially if that win meant more life together. I had convinced myself that I loved him. After all, he was my closest friend. I agreed to the organizational change in the spirit of believing in my friend. But there was something different about the feeling of what was happening in that office. I wasn't smart enough to put it together in the moment. I would soon learn how complicated friendship can be, and how much my love was lacking.

Since that day, I have spent a lot of time thinking about the beauty of God eternally existing in three distinct but equal persons. The mystery that the great theologians have coined the Trinity. God the Father, God the Son, and God the Spirit exist in pure, unadulterated love for one another at the core of all existence. No want. No need. Just the peace of His self-expressed *I AM*-ness being constantly volleyed back and forth between them. Sheer communal perfection is the primary building block for everything we know and see. It's something that pushes the wisest of us to the edge of our comprehension. But, if it wasn't so . . . if He wasn't so, life as we know it would fall apart. I believe in God existing in three persons. I would even say that Him being that way is something that I desperately need. I'm also struck by how different our relational lives can be from His reality. True unity is rare. Strife, jealousy, and war are more common than not, on both a global and personal scale. Something must have gone horribly wrong to get us where we are. If I'm honest, I live in a constant state of comparison, and I'm not the only one.

The next three years were the perfect storm. The complexity of fallen humanity in ego and insecurity in brute force. It was an onslaught from every direction. I can honestly say I had never been so internally disoriented in my life. I will try my best to unpack all the factors at play, but even now it's difficult to fully understand. At the time, the church was about thirty years old. The full-time staff approached 350 or so to support the weight of the 18,000-20,000 people that would attend one of the six campuses every week (five of which Ben and I had helped to launch during our tenure).

The founding pastor had led the congregation faithfully from its inception. No small feat. I can't imagine the things he encountered during those three decades of leadership. He had the tough demeanor of a defensive coordinator, which led to a "life coach" approach from the pulpit and a cutting sarcasm in the office. His motivation was to make Christianity relevant to influential men who fit a certain cultural stereotype, with the hope that their impact would ripple down to the broader community. He was a very strategic leader with a low tolerance for sideways energy. He and his team had even gone so far as to create a fictional target character to focus the energies of the church's reach. They had given him a name and built his personality by picking out appealing ads in popular men's periodicals. The character had a wife and a couple of kids, all with their own names. They filtered their evangelism strategy through his lens, asking "Would this appeal to. . .?

The church's approach was attractional in nature. Meaning they wanted to attract a particular kind of person. Its ministry philosophy was highly informed by the strong influence of other mega churches that came to the forefront of the evangelical subculture in the late 1980s and early 1990s. The main idea was that the last thing our cities needed was another "church." Church in that sense of the word was a synonym for irrelevant. It was thought of in the pejorative. All of this came from a strong desire to see people come to know Jesus—a very good thing.

As a result of its ever-increasing size, the executive pastoral staff, made up of successful businessmen, had a strong leaning toward focusing the full-time employees on leadership development, organizational health, and mission alignment. This is very common for large organizations that strive to retain culture through corporate methods. The content of meetings consisted largely of lessons gleaned from the current issue of the Harvard Business Review or the latest breaking books on leadership or hospitality. The thrust of the church's energy was geared toward steady, quantifiable growth in attendance, baptisms, and giving year over year. The pastor had a knack for motivating people toward that end, and the church's consistent growth was the clear result.

I am aware that I may be painting an incomplete picture of this place with my language. I admit my bias as I don't remember it in the rosiest of ways. The truth is all churches are one hundred percent comprised of sinners . . . like me. There were some beautiful people who had experienced major life changes through the ministry of this church. Some of the truest sense of community Ashley and I had ever experienced in our lives together occurred as a result of our time there. But even now, as I describe the culture of this church, I realize how foreign it was to what I had previously known. I was a feeler. Still am. A true Enneagram 4, if you're into that sort of thing. But I'm also an intellectual. I tend to feel comfortable in the deep end of the thought pool, constantly wrestling with the *why* behind the *what*. I drift toward waxing philosophical with the force of gravity. That didn't bode well in a high-doing-over-being culture that measured its effectiveness by standards of practicality. Add to that a fiery tip-the-temple-tables prophetic angst toward unfaithfulness to Biblical authority, and you've got me pegged. Seeing the pulpit leveraged as a platform for sharing tips and tricks for winning at life in the place of the proclamation of gospel truth made my skin crawl. I was destined to be at odds with my surroundings during my time there. But up to this point, I wasn't in it alone. I found deep consolation in sharing my frustrations and concerns with Ben, and he was a great listener. For the most part, we were taking things in from the same angle.

Things got more complicated. It became very apparent that the pastor questioned my level of "manliness" and doubted my ability to appeal to his target audience as a worship leader. In this model of ministry, music was a consumer entity. Worship seemed to be an afterthought. There was a divorce between the two, and the former was simply a means to the end of getting the right people in the seats to hit the desired growth metrics. Case in point, my voice was too high. My emotions were too deep and on my sleeve. To him, I was off-putting to the average Joe. I didn't fit the algorithm, but according to the pastor, Ben did. His voice was deeper, his build was stronger, and his approach was less emotional. We had never been pitted against each other until this point. It felt like wearing a straitjacket and being thrown into a swimming pool. On one particular occasion, while Ben and I were standing next to each other, the pastor casually walked up, nodded at Ben, and said jokingly, "Well, it looks like we've finally got a *man's man* of a worship leader around here." My father wounds festered at the words. At that moment, I didn't realize how much damage they had done.

Ben's promotion, coupled with the pervading culture, began to unveil the worst part of who I was. It simultaneously exploited the flaws in my character and pulled the covers off the imperfection of my love for my friend. It was like a double-barreled shotgun pointed at my chest. There were nights that I sat up in my bed, seething with jealousy over Ben being embraced by the leaders there. We were being pulled apart. There were invitations to Christmas parties at the executive pastor's house, and trips to conferences in different parts of the country. Each new twist would add another layer to my envy. It was frightening to my wife. It was frightening to me.

All of this was just from my side. I can't speak with any level of clarity on what was happening in Ben's mind and heart, but I know for a fact that it wasn't easy. I imagine there were many restless nights he wrestled with the expectations placed on him as a leader and how they might impact our friendship. I'm sure he prayed that he would handle it well. It was a cauldron of confusion. The intimacy of our friendship was being hijacked by a corporate giant. The simplicity and innocence of a beautiful brotherhood had suffered a hostile takeover. If the conversation in that little office was taking a bite out of a forbidden fruit, this was living east of Eden. The more I came to Ben with my frustrations and grievances about the church's culture, the more he had to distance himself from me. I wanted to discuss it with him. I wanted him to look at me and say, "I know, man." But the conversations couldn't pan out that way. I put him at a crossroads. It was a matter of loyalty to me or corporate alignment. The pressures on him from the top were doing the same thing from the opposite direction. The implications of the struggle were becoming increasingly apparent: jobs, livelihoods, and relationships. We had both picked up and moved our entire worlds to the desert, and at this point, we had spent valuable years building this worship ministry *together*. However, something was going to have to give.

CHAPTER 7

While the tension was building, we continued to lead worship in one of the largest churches in the country on a weekly basis. But I began to experience physical symptoms of anxiety every time I put my guitar on and stood in front of a microphone. I was shutting down. The Gibson wasn't even enough to console me. I remember Easter Sunday morning 2015, standing in front of 55,000 people at the University of Phoenix Stadium with the heaviness of it all pressing down on my shoulders. Ben stood to my right. My head was spinning. I did my best to keep myself together, but I was unraveling. It took faith to verbally profess the reality of the resurrection in song that morning. I'm sure it did for Ben, too.

The executive pastor at the church had some understanding of the complexity of what was going on. He took the steps that good organizational leaders take to try to mitigate the situation—counseling, time off, etc. But they only delayed the inevitable. His intentions were good, but it felt like he was trying to heal the deep wound of the soul with corporate management tactics. We were speaking different languages. At one point, he looked at me and said something like, "I want to be like a brother to you in this." My immediate reaction was, "I had a brother, and you took him." You can't assume the intimacy that two decades of relational equity bring that quickly. I was too hurt to let him do that.

My gut tells me that there were conversations among key leaders in a room with a big wooden table that led Ben to make the decision he made. But it's hard for me not to be cynical about it. He called me to a meeting at a coffee shop across the street from the church. We sat down at a bistro table outside the front door. There were a few beats of quiet. We were both grieving the loss of something precious. We didn't need any words to realize it. He broke the silence as sensitively as he could, knowing the full weight of what he was about to say. I knew there was a place in his heart where he truly believed he was doing the right thing for me. He knew I was dying, but a lot of what was killing me was coming directly from him.

By the time we were done, I walked away with six months' severance and a broken heart. There was no possible way for me to think of it as anything but complete betrayal. The closer the friend, the deeper the wound. That's just the way it is. I drove home to tell Ashley what had happened. It was a divorce, or like cutting off a limb, or maybe cutting out a heart. The collateral damage was widespread. Our friends and the large family of musicians we had invested in over the years tried to console us without taking sides, like confused children in a custody battle. The entire community felt the ripple effect. It was devastating.

The next six months felt like purgatory. Around every corner, there were big questions wrought with pain. Where were we going to go? What were we going to do? Who were we going to love? God had graced us with a small, extremely tight-knit group of friends who felt like family. They had become so important to us through the season in which we found ourselves. Jordan and Lauren Messer, Joey and Amy Cassidy, all with their young kids, whom my boys considered their brothers and sisters. When we had moved to Phoenix six years prior, we had discovered that our three families had all relocated there from Nashville within a few months of one another. There was an instant connection that bound us together.

In this season, we leaned on them hard, and they loved us as we weathered the storm together. The six of us shared many meals and late nights under the desert stars, trying to make sense of what was happening. In many ways, they were just as confused and hurt as we were. Jordan and Lauren lived just down the street from us. Their consistent presence and tenderness of heart were an invaluable gift. We needed people to call our own. They were those people. Their extended family adopted us, inviting us for Mother's Day and Easter dinners. In their generosity toward us, we never had to wonder who we would celebrate with, or who we would weep with. Our affection for them grew through intimate conversations that we shared, bearing each other's burdens. But along the way, we started to come to a brutal realization. The domino that tipped when Ben let me go would likely result in the loss of sharing life with them too. The losses seemed to grow exponentially, compounding on one another. We didn't want to leave them.

I wanted to stay in Phoenix. I tried to figure out how to make a living in a way that would allow us to keep our tight-knit community together. As I did, there was an odd tug of war between the practicalities of finding ways to pay our mortgage and the calling I knew I had to engage in the ministerial field. Up until this point, these things hadn't been at odds with one another. I tried to picture myself doing something vocational that didn't involve using my hands and my heart to admonish the church. The thought was disorienting. I spent weeks in a dizzying haze, reaching out for anything that looked remotely like an opportunity to stay put.

A month after I was let go, such an opportunity arose. I received a call from a local worship leader in the area who had been an acquaintance of mine. He was aware of the difficulty that Ashley and I were facing. He asked how we were doing, and I told him the truth. I was confused, hurt, and looking for what was next. He offered his condolences for what had happened, and I thanked him for his kindness. He then began to unpack the reason for the call. An opportunity had come across his path, and it made him think of me. Even before he began unpacking what it was about, my heart began to jump to the premature conclusion that this might be God's provision for the Olsons to stay in Phoenix. I was desperate, and my desperation was taking a toll on my ability to remain objective.

I listened as he described a unique church that was about to be planted in Scottsdale. As he spoke, I noticed that his words had a calculated and cryptic feel to them, as if he was restraining himself from fully disclosing something. Aware of my own desperation, I kept myself from asking too many questions as well. The phone call felt a little like a poker game with neither party wanting to show the completeness of their hand. By the time it was over, I had agreed to meet with the church planter a few days later at a Panera on the north side of the city. After I hung up the phone, I described the conversation to Ashley. We both shared the desire to stay in the desert with the people that we loved, and she was intrigued by the call. But as I described the conversation, she shared my lack of clarity on what it was about.

On the morning of February 1, 2016, I made the twenty-minute drive from our home to the Desert Ridge town center off the 101 for the meeting. After parking my car, I walked through the door of the Panera and shook hands with Mark Driscoll.

For the next hour, we became acquainted with one another over cheap coffee and pastries. I was somewhat aware of who Mark was and what he had been through. Honestly, it would have been nearly impossible not to be. Much of it had been the fodder for national headlines, making it hard to miss. For the better part of two years, Mark had been the official lightning rod of evangelical Christianity. An office that few aspire to. Much of what he had experienced had overflowed from the small subculture of American megachurch Christendom into the mainstream. I don't think he had reached the status of a household name, but he wasn't far off. He had also become the face of toxic masculinity in the evangelical church, something that had already taken a toll on me. Ironically, I knew that the founding pastor of CCV had spent time with Mark up in Seattle discussing the ins and outs of what it means to be a church for men, which was a big part of how his influence pulled Ben and me apart. To say I was still raw from what had happened at CCV would be an understatement. It was the most unlikely of meetings. By that time, Mark had spent twenty-four months living largely underground in North Phoenix with his family, displaced from the melee at Mars Hill. Naturally, I was curious to meet the man personally. He had achieved celebrity status in the most unorthodox of ways.

As we shared our stories with one another, I instantly noticed the air of confidence he carried. He was naturally inclined toward having answers to questions, and he made a lot of sense when he gave them to me. He was incredibly articulate and clear. I tried to imagine all he had experienced up to that point and how it informed who he was as he sat in front of me at the table. I had zero chance of being even mildly successful at it. By this time, I was aware of the impact that painful experiences could have on someone. I was in the middle of one. His journey had evolved on such a grand scale. It gave me a sense of perspective on what I was going through. For example, the day we met was the same day the website for his new church, Trinity Church, went live. He told me how grateful he was that it was also the day Obama's results in the Iowa Caucuses would grab the national headlines, allowing him to fade into the background. For as much pain as I was carrying with Ben, I didn't share nearly those types of concerns.

I told him what had happened at CCV. He listened quietly and intently, and when I was done, he told me how sorry he was about what had happened. He said it from a place of deep empathy and awareness of what that kind of hurt feels like. I could tell he knew about CCV and what made it and other churches like it tick. He offered some of his thoughts on it. They were absolutely brilliant. He was respectful in his delivery, yet forward-thinking. Like a courtroom attorney, he systematically unpacked a doctrinal disconnect in the way they operated. He described the danger of religious activity being carried out unrooted from a sense of God's character and nature as described in His Word. The more I considered what he said, the more it made sense to me. I found myself agreeing with him. After a few twists and turns, the conversation began to center on the theme of forgiveness and its importance. He recognized how hurt I was. He knew what we were there to talk about, but his pastoral instincts gravitated toward leading me down a path of dealing with the hurt before we got into any of that. He offered some of what he had experienced since leaving Mars Hill. I was grateful for his words. By the time the conversation ended, I had accepted his offer for Ashley and me to join him and his wife, Grace, in a Bible study on forgiveness at their home.

A few weeks later, we pulled up to their place and rang the doorbell. We were greeted at the front door and warmly welcomed into their home. Most of their kids were home at the time, giving the place a lively feeling. As I saw them in the house, I tried to wrap my head around the conversations they had shared as a family over the previous two years. They had been uprooted from their Seattle home, where they had spent most of their lives. His kids had left all that was familiar to them in the wake of what had happened at Mars Hill. Now, all was different: schools, weather, relationships, and . . . church. I'm not entirely sure what I perceived was accurate, but I thought I caught a sense of guardedness in the air. Here they were, on the cusp of a new venture in church planting after two years of recovery. They had to be aware of the prospect of Ashley and me joining them on the journey. As I processed it, I recognized the guardedness I was developing in response to my own hurt. It all made sense. I thought about our situation and my kids, wondering what life would look like for us on the other end of the transition we had just begun. I wondered if part of it would include sharing life and ministry with Mark and his family. We exchanged the usual small talk about how difficult it is to keep the house clean while the kids are running about the place. I motioned toward the five or six Nerf bullets that I had noticed lying about the living room. Mark smiled and offered in response, "It's not a museum." I knew he had said it before.

Ashley and I joined Mark and Grace around their kitchen table. With glasses of water and Bibles open, Mark began to pore through passages on forgiveness.

Mark contextualized Jesus's parables and Paul's words of instruction to where Ashley and I found ourselves, and to where he and Grace had been. He spoke compassionately but authoritatively. As his thoughts ended, he spoke about the potential destruction of living in unforgiveness. Unforgiveness opens the door to the demonic in our lives. As he spoke, I thought about the graveness of the assertion he had made. I thought about how angry I had been. Memories of being overcome by fits of rage at Ben floated to the front of my mind. Mark was persuasive in how he presented his words. It was as if he was trying to sell us something, but I don't think he was wrong. I think he believed it and that he had applied it to his own heart. At the time, I was so caught up in my own pain and how what he said applied to it that I hadn't considered how it also applied to what happened to my dad.

Over the next few weeks, I continued to meet with Mark. Amidst conversations about healing from what we had been through, we continued to entertain the possibility of my joining him at Trinity. I met a few families that had moved with him and Grace to Phoenix. I could tell that they had been beaten up by what had happened as well. They looked at Mark as a leader and a pastor and were committed to helping him in his new endeavor. Through every exchange, I tried to picture myself in community with them, asking myself if these were the people that God intended for us to partner with in ministry in the season ahead. I weighed all of it with Ashley and my strong desire to stay connected with the Messers and the Cassidys and to watch our kids grow up together. We pushed ourselves to do our best and try to see clearly through all the emotions we had. It seemed impossible.

Mark had somehow managed to raise the funds to purchase a building for the church, located a few blocks off the 101 in central Scottsdale. To say it was bizarre would be an understatement. The building was intended to be a church from its conception, but it had been vacant for years. When Mark showed it to me for the first time, it had a post-apocalyptic feel to it. It looked like the house that Luke Skywalker had grown up in on the planet Tatooine. The imposing structure sat on a piece of land that hadn't been properly paid attention to for a decade, overgrown with desert weeds and strewn with tumbleweed. It was a bright white cement dome built in the 1960s in mid-century modern design. The architect who designed it had also worked on the Crystal Cathedral in Los Angeles for Robert Schuller. This structure shared some of the same oddities and eccentricities. It had a large gravel parking lot on its east side, where parishioners used to pull up and tune in to the sermon broadcast from their own vehicles over the AM radio waves. At the time, it was a groundbreaking concept. It looked like a drive-in movie theater without the screen. It was everything you loved about church from the comfort of your Oldsmobile. There was a door from the platform inside the church that led directly to a balcony overlooking the parking lot. After the final prayer, the founding pastor would walk out the door and wave to the folks in the parking lot like the Pope at Saint Peter's, blessing them as they drove away.

Its oddness resonated with Mark. He looked at it and saw potential. Mark had already been meeting with a core of people for a weekly Bible study in the building in its disheveled state. He and his small team were organizing workdays, empowering those interested in bringing the place back to life. I took them up on it on a few occasions. I pulled weeds, painted walls, and prayed.

A few weeks into our relationship, Mark approached me about leading worship at one of the weekend gatherings. It was billed as one of the first official gatherings of Trinity Fellowship. In an effort to keep putting one foot in front of the other, I agreed to it. To my knowledge, they hadn't incorporated corporate singing in their gatherings to that point. Mark and I spent some time discussing the role that the arts would play at Trinity. He had strong opinions about the culture he wanted to create. Many of which were informed by the successes that he had experienced at Mars Hill, which was known for its gritty authenticity. As he spoke about it, I wondered if I could share his vision. The last thing I wanted to do was find myself in a position of public leadership in a church setting where I was at odds with another strong visionary leader. In the end, Mark didn't micromanage the process. Instead, he adopted a posture of gratitude and excitement at the prospect of people singing worship songs to God under the cement dome. I prepared as I had so many weekends before and showed up early the following Sunday to lead.

Approximately 150 people showed up at Trinity that morning. That number doesn't include a handful of picketers who paraded with sandwich board signs and blowhorns just off the property line. People filtered through the doors into the main worship space under the giant cement dome. There was a sense of excitement in the room, and many people there seemed ready to engage in the vision that Mark was beginning to set before them. I recognized a few faces from CCV. My wife and kids were there, as were the Cassidys and the Messers. I felt a lump begin to form in my throat as I saw them sitting together in the same row. I stood just behind Mark with the Gibson hung over my shoulder. He opened the service and highlighted the fact that this would be the first service in which the people of Trinity Church would sing together. He bowed his head and led everyone in prayer. I kept my eyes open to watch the people respond to his words, wondering what was about to happen. After Mark's closing amen, I stepped to the microphone, took my hands to the Gibson's neck, and began to sing the lyrics to the song Good, Good Father: "I've heard a thousand stories of what they think you're like, but I've heard the tender whispers of love in the dead of night, and they tell me that you're pleased and that I'm never alone . . . "

The words landed heavy on my bruised heart. The sound billowed through the round room and off the domed cement roof. It was just the Gibson and my voice, but the uncontrollable acoustics of the place made it seem like an arena. By the time we hit the chorus, people in the seats had started to join in. I caught Ashley and my boys out of the corner of my eye. Then Joey and Jordan. The lump in my throat began to grow just like the sound bouncing off the walls. By the time we hit the bridge, I couldn't hold it together.

"You are perfect in all of your ways." My voice cracked as I choked back the tears. I looked down at Mark. There he was the most outspoken proponent for the "dewussification" of the American church with tears streaming down his cheeks. I never pictured William Wallace as a weeper, but something crept up on him that Sunday morning. As it turned out, the room was full of hurting people who needed to be reminded of the tenderness of God's fatherly heart, like my wife, the Cassidys, and the Messers. I certainly did, and apparently, Mark and Grace did too. We barely made it through the rest of the set. At the end of the time of worship, Mark got up with tears in his eyes and confessed that his emotions were getting the best of him. He had, without a doubt, been brought to a place of reflection on all that had transpired in his family's life to bring them to that Sunday at Trinity, where God had led them and provided along the way.

The severance clock ticked as we continued to try to find our footing. Ashley and I shared the weight of prayer and seeking what would be next. It was a heavy weight to bear. Amidst all the thoughts and emotions surrounding our departure from CCV, our close community in Phoenix, and what was happening with Mark, we were steeped in confusion.

That week, I showed up at Trinity for a workday. I greeted the other people who had arrived to help around the property. We talked about the Sunday morning service together and how impactful the time of worship had been.

I felt conflicted. Bruises were still forming on my heart as a result of bearing it so regularly in worship at CCV and the way I felt I had been handled in return. Stepping up to do the same in a foreign place under a leader like Mark was daunting. After a short time of prayer, we were divided into small groups and assigned tasks. My group stayed under the cement dome. I grabbed a vacuum cleaner and an extension cord and began pushing it back and forth through the aisles between the seats, picking up what Sunday morning had left. As my arm swung back and forth and the sound of the vacuum rushed and waned, I had a conversation with the Lord. The white noise purring from the vacuum acted like an isolation booth. I pulled away from the rest of the people, finding a patch of carpet on the outskirts of the giant, round room. I spoke out loud, but softly, "God, what are you up to?" My eyes scanned the room. I looked at the unfamiliar faces as they went about their assigned work. "God, help me here. Is this it? Is this where you want us?"

I saw the two gentlemen who had moved from Seattle to work with Mark. I thought of how complicated it had gotten working in a church setting with Ben. "Are these the guys? Is this who I'm supposed to jump back in the foxhole with?" I saw Mark giving directions to some folks on the other side of the room. "God, is this my pastor?" It wasn't audible, but it was clear. He responded, "*No*". I clicked the vacuum back into its full and upright position and stepped on the on/off switch with the toe of my running shoe. I walked out the back door of the cement dome into the blinding Phoenix sunshine, climbed in the car, and drove home.

I called Mark a few days later and officially passed on Trinity. Ashley and I knew that phone call would lead to us not living five houses down from Lauren and Jordan and being only a fifteen-minute drive from the Cassidys. But jumping on with Mark wasn't the right thing to do.

A word about Mark Driscoll, based on my firsthand experience. Through our time together, I could see how hurt he had been from what had happened in Seattle. He recognized how hurt I was, and he offered sound pastoral advice. I could see the shadows of his immense confidence, of his quickness to give answers. I could see how his personality would lend itself to what had transpired at Mars Hill. But here's the thing, Mark never took advantage of me. He had ample opportunity, given the frame of mind and heart I was in at the time.

As I look back, I'm amazed at this part of my journey. The irony of God in allowing it all to happen the way it did. There I was, unknowingly walking in the wake of woundedness from what the enemy had done to my father, fresh off the face of that same enemy's brutal exploitation of a friendship of the most intimate kind by means of pride and power from all parties, and all this in the context of the church. In the middle of that kind of fray, God in His sovereignty saw to it that I was cared for by none other than Mark Driscoll, whose state of heart and mind at the time I will leave to the imagination of the reader, with the sole caution to tread lightly.

What can you make of this? The cognitive dissonance in it can knock a man over. Here's a thought for your consideration: *it's grace*. It's paradoxical, defying human reason. How can God use deeply flawed and imperfect people to care for other deeply flawed and imperfect people? Even more confounding than that, how can God, in His ultimate perfection and holy otherness, find Himself in the company of deeply flawed and imperfect people? Why would He do this? I've spent a great deal of time wrestling with these kinds of questions. Here's where the wrestle has led me. They only find their resolution in the mystery of the person of Jesus Christ. He is divinity wrapped in humanity, offered for the sake of the brokenness of the world. In his letter to the church at Colossae, the Apostle Paul describes Jesus as one who "holds all things together" (Col. 1:17). Paul goes on to describe Him as the head of the church, Jesus's body.

When I think about Mark and me huddled around cheap coffee and pastries at the Desert Ridge Panera in north Scottsdale, it offers a pretty good picture of what the church is. Two wounded people finding healing, connection, and missional purpose in Christ while on the journey. The church, whether large and influential (like Mars Hill, CCV, or Eleven22) or small and modest (like the saints gathered in small numbers under persecution around the world), does well to be reminded of this beautiful simplicity.

CHAPTER 8

Around that same time, a friend from my Nashville days reached out to me, unaware of what we were going through. We previously met at a small church plant we were both involved in while living there. He was the service programming director, and I led worship under his direction when I wasn't out on the road with Michael. During that season, we spent some time discipling a small group of young, talented musicians who played in the church band. As we led them through the book of Hebrews, we discovered a shared affinity for how we felt ministry should be approached.

After I left Nashville for Phoenix, he relocated down to Atlanta to join the staff of a church similar to the one where I ended up. Oddly enough, he had experienced some similar tensions there, minus the whole 'having your manhood questioned by the lead pastor and being let go by your best friend' part. His prophetic angst had led him to Jacksonville, Florida, where he had connected on a heart level with the vision of Pastor Joby Martin. He was serving under Joby as the executive pastor of The Church of Eleven22. At the time, I didn't get the name but have since grown to love its meaning.

It was hard for me to think clearly about anything amidst the circumstances we were facing, but there was something about his description of what was happening at the church that resonated with me. I told him what we had been through. It probably should have given him some pause, but it didn't. He was a natural-born risk-taker. God had laid me on his heart regarding Eleven22, and he was going to see it through. He asked if I would be willing to come down and check it out. In need of some direction for what was next, I grabbed the guitar and jumped on a flight.

To say that Eleven22 was different from what I had experienced at CCV would be a drastic understatement. The church met in a gutted-out Walmart in the armpit of a stereotypical north Florida strip mall. It looked like it was being held together by duct tape and band-aids, but it had soul. When I walked in, I experienced an eclectic mixture of Bohemian surf culture and redneck flair. It was equal parts surfboards and flipflops to pick-up trucks and taxidermy. It was authentic. There was a freshness to the feel of it, and there was something in the eyes of the people that stirred my broken heart, specifically Joby's.

We sat across the table from one another at a local sandwich shop that had previously doubled as his office. He unpacked the history of how he ended up where he was. I did the same. He had eyes like a shark. I could see a passion for the glory of God to be made known through the unique expression of a doctrinally sound, Spirit-infused local church. He was a pastor, and I needed one. My heart was still very fragile, but it leaped a little bit as he cast the vision. He's a master at casting vision. The mission statement of the place read like a solution to the tensions that had haunted me in the desert. No target audiences, no separation of discipleship and evangelism, no "worship" as a means to another end. Just a deep desire to see the living Word of God at work, bearing fruit in souls saved and disciples made.

They offered me a job, but I turned it down—twice. I'm not joking. We didn't want to leave what was familiar to us. Change is hard, especially when you're in pain—ask post-exodus Israel. They stood on the other side of a parted sea and still felt the tug to go backward. Just because God is at work and the kingdom of heaven is advancing in your life doesn't mean it won't hurt like . . . well, like hell.

My experience tells me that pain and maturity often walk hand in hand. "For it was fitting that he, for whom and by whom all things exist, in bringing many sons to glory, should make the founder of their salvation perfect through suffering" (Hebrews 2:10). Hate to say it, but it's true. Suffering is often the unwelcome means of sanctification. Anyone who tells you otherwise is lying.

It took a minute, but we finally gave in and embraced the change. It was right, but there was nothing about it that felt good. Joey Cassidy, who happened to be a realtor, helped us list our Phoenix home. Much like the trip out, my father-in-law and I packed up the Toyota Sequoia (we upgraded to the third row as the family grew) with the essentials, including my two oldest sons and the Gibson, and headed back east. Ashley and the baby would follow by plane. As we pulled out of the driveway, I tried to push through the loss. I remember it beginning to rain as I waved goodbye to Jordan and Lauren. It never rains in Phoenix. They shrank in my rear-view mirror as we drove away. I didn't say goodbye to Ben. That would have been too difficult for both of us.

Eleven22 was like God's manna for us. That doesn't mean that it immediately felt like home. It didn't. You really can't microwave a sense of home. But it nourished my heart, which desperately needed the healing. The way Joby opened the Scriptures was like air to me. Ashley and I would routinely reach out and grab each other's hands while listening on Sunday mornings as if to say, *This is what was missing*.

At the front of the stage, there were altar benches made out of reclaimed wood. They were used routinely as folks wrestled with what God was doing in their hearts. This was the kind of place where it was okay if you weren't completely okay. We weren't, but God's grace unleashed in the good news of Jesus was pervasive. It felt good to have a dedicated place to pray in church. I used those altar benches when I could. I loved leading worship there, which I did frequently—me and the Gibson. It sounded as good in Jacksonville as it did everywhere else. I don't want to be overdramatic about it, but the familiarity of having it hanging from my shoulder helped my state of mind.

Chapter 8

I'd be lying if I said the pace of growth at Eleven22 allowed me time to fully recover from what had happened in Phoenix before getting my hands dirty again. The six months of severance Ben slid across the coffee shop bistro table were a blessing, but those six months were the farthest thing from rest. They were weighed down by the heavy lifting of grief and change. My new leaders expressed their desire for me to have some time to heal, but it wasn't in the cards. The Church of Eleven22 was a fast-moving bullet train. But there was a palpable presence of God in the work that truly sustained me along the way. Jesus once described a kind of soul food that occurs as a result of being about the Father's business. I guess this felt like that. In many ways, the practical side of getting started at Eleven22 felt oddly similar to what it was like in Phoenix. There was trust to build, problems to solve, and systems to implement to accommodate rapid growth. That rate of growth was similar to where I had come from, but the culture couldn't have been more different.

I didn't have a partner. When I thought about it, sadness would roll in like an ocean wave. It was the first time that Ashley and I really felt alone. We knew that we weren't really alone, but it felt like we were. You can be alone in a crowd. In some ways, that kind of alone can feel more acute than the deserted island kind of alone. We spent many nights crying together on our living room couch as we processed the deep loss. There was a yearning in both of us for familiar faces, but there weren't any around. No recognizable eyes to peer into, other than each other's. Amidst all God was doing in and through us in our new home, there was an unavoidable valley of grief to pass through (see Psalm 23). As I look back, I know that He was with us through that valley. There are times when He, in perfectly pure kindness, strips away the familiar to build a deep sense of dependence on Him. It's in those times when the roots of faith grow sturdier. The tears might even water those roots. We watered them a lot.

There is a unique kind of camaraderie that comes as a result of years spent making music together. Of all the things that were lost in the fray, that's what I missed most—the brotherhood part. I couldn't explain it, but when Ben used his gift, a part of me would come alive. There were times when he would get completely absorbed in it. I would smile as I watched it go down. It made him come alive as well. That experience had been a regular occurrence in my life for decades, twenty years or so. When you experience something like that for that long, you develop a sense of dependency on it. It's subliminal. I wasn't realizing it when it happened, but that dependency had grown steadily over the years. It disappeared so abruptly; I was in withdrawal.

When Ashley and I moved to Florida, I was unaware that Eleven22 had a relationship with a couple of acquaintances of mine from my Nashville days. Shane & Shane, known to me now as "B" and "E" (Barnard & Everitt), had been a part of some artist showcases back in my record deal days. The first time I had ever seen those guys was when I was in Bible school. I'm almost certain that Ben and I bought tickets to an acoustic show they performed in another Christian college in town. That was around the same time they were starting their journey together as well.

I remember it being an amazing night. After that show, I walked around the third floor of my college dorm and watched fellow students try to do that crazy fast acoustic strumming thing that B does. None of them could do it. I still can't do it.

In terms of sheer experience of camaraderie and brotherhood in worship ministry over the long haul, Shane & Shane would be near the top of the list, if not number one. Ironically, God saw fit for our paths to cross more often now that I was in Jacksonville at Eleven22. They had known Ben and had previously worked with him on various projects. They knew we both had a stint playing for Michael W., and that we had moved to Phoenix together. When they were in town, I shared an abbreviated version of some of the heartache that we had been through. As I worked my way through describing how I had ended up in Jacksonville, I could see the empathy build in their eyes. They both instinctively knew what had happened was a game-changer, probably because they could relate to the complexities of brotherhood and ministry.

Seeing B and E brought a smile to my face. Hearing them brought a bigger one, especially when it was in my in-ear mix. Whenever we had the chance to lead worship together, a feeling of home would come back. That was God's grace. B fell in love with the Gibson—head over heels, which is saying a lot. Few guys can wield that instrument the way he can. Any hint at an endorsement from his lips would carry quite a bit of weight. At one point, he actually said playing that guitar was like "playing a saber of light." He wanted it: I could tell.

Whereas B is the beating heart of Shane & Shane, E is the entrepreneurial genius. Don't let him fool you. He doesn't talk much with a microphone in front of his face, but he knows how to make things happen. A super savvy dude wired for procurement and global domination. And he can sing unnaturally high without working hard at all. (Sidenote: The fact that these two guys found each other the way they did and what they've done is proof of the existence of God. They are like two nine-foot Steinway grand pianos dovetailed together. One is amazing on its own, but two is next level.)

E immediately moved into business mode on the Gibson. I recall a specific Sunday morning when it became particularly intense. B stood center stage, leading Eleven22 in song with the guitar. It was a beautiful moment, and we were lost in it. I was stage-right behind a keyboard, trying to keep up. E was moving subtly between us with a microphone in hand, vocals blazing out from under the perfectly curved bill of his patch hat. While B was praying to close out the worship set, his partner moved toward me with an intense look in his eyes. I could tell he wanted to say something. I was prepped for the profound. As he leaned over, I took my left in-ear monitor out and heard him whisper, "Dude, I have so much cash . . .." Then he walked away. In all transparency, I briefly considered the amount of money it would take for me to give up the Gibson, but I quickly realized that it was an exercise in futility. Letting it go would be like losing an old friend, and I wasn't in the place to handle that sort of thing.

The time spent in Jacksonville in the early years felt like being caught in a tug-of-war. God graciously afforded our family to be involved in one of the most life-giving expressions of the local church that I had ever seen in Eleven22. Yet we felt the tug of sadness from what happened in Phoenix. I know living in the past isn't good for anyone. I didn't want to get stuck in that, but it didn't feel like healing was going to be instantaneous either.

Substantive movements of the soul tend to take some time. There are Bible verses that speak directly to what happens to a man when he's double-minded. *Instability* is the word. There have been days when that word could describe me as I've moved through ministry and life. It's also not surprising that God has been gracious in using me, despite myself. He is merciful. But at times, the emotional extremes can be disorienting. From feeling the exhilaration of walking out into the Atlantic Ocean to be a part of seeing 1900 plus people declare their faith in Jesus through baptism, to moments of introspective reflection on all that has transpired to get my family and me to where we are. You can get dizzy from that sort of thing, especially if you tend to process things emotionally like I do.

I could see the deep truth of the instability that comes from double-mindedness starting to surface in my life experience at that time. God was allowing me to become increasingly more self-aware. As time passed, I could feel His Spirit pulling my heart toward the things that my mind knew needed to happen—forgiveness and reconciliation. It's easy to say those words, to relate to them conceptually. It's much harder to internalize them on a heart level and to embody them. I could make the argument that it's impossible to do in one's own strength.

About two years into my time at Eleven22, I was invited to travel to Israel. It was a once-in-a-lifetime opportunity. I was one of about fifty, most of whom were church members and attendees. We took a pilgrimage together following the life of Jesus. God's word came alive to us as we walked where He had walked.

While on the trip, I sat on the north bank of the Sea of Galilee and listened as a fellow Eleven22 staffer gave a brilliant teaching on Jesus's reinstatement of Peter in John 21. I sat and listened to the teaching, where it is commonly believed that the conversation actually occurred. It was surreal. It's a familiar story. The passage ends with Jesus extending an invitation to Peter. Really, it was a gracious command with unbelievably immense consequences weighing in the balance. It just so happened to be the same gracious command that he had offered when they first met, even though he had willfully denied him three times. "Follow me," Jesus said. It must have stung when Peter heard those words again. That kind of grace doesn't make sense. Peter had to see himself through Jesus's eyes to be able to accept His offer.

The teaching ended with the question, "What do you need to let go of in your past in order to move into what God has called you to in your future?" To me, the application was obvious. I winced as I thought about it. As a tangible expression of our answer, we were challenged to pick up a rock from the Galilee shoreline and chuck it into the water to symbolize that we were moving on. I didn't want to do it, but I knew I had to.

After the teaching was over, I sat quietly for a while stewing on what was being asked. There was a wrestling match in my spirit. I gave in and mustered the courage to stand up and grab a rock from the water's edge. I said a prayer of release and hurled it into the very lake on which Jesus had walked a few thousand years prior.

I can't say that I felt anything particularly significant. I don't believe that God owed me any sort of existential moment as I let that rock fly, but it was a step in the right direction. A good friend of mine, whom I had confided in about what had happened in Phoenix and had lifted me up in prayer, saw me do it. He subtly walked up beside me and stood quietly for a moment. We stood there together, blanketed in the Israeli sunshine, barefoot in the Sea of Galilee. When the silence felt like it needed to end, I squinted forward over the glistening water and said, "I threw the rock." He said, "I saw that." (Charles has a way with words.) He put his arm around my shoulder and we headed back to the bus.

It's hard to describe, but as time passed, I began to be able to wrap my thoughts and emotions around the totality of the loss Ashley and I had experienced. In the first few years after we left the desert, it was overwhelming to process everything at once. One aspect of it would trigger another. Things would snowball quickly. It took all the discipline I had to lock things down so I wouldn't drown. Time brought perspective, perspective brought understanding. I began to see both the circumstances in which I had been and who I was becoming on the other side of them more clearly. God was working, and the knowledge that He was near was beautiful. I was reminded that I was a sheep and He was *my* Shepherd.

CHAPTER 9

In the late summer of 2020, Pastor Joby announced to the staff that the main thrust of 2021 would be relationships. He said he felt God leading us to spend twenty-four weeks moving through the Gospel of John, verse by verse, taking a deep look at Jesus to discover how we should relate to each other in response to His love. This excited me. I love the book of John—always have. Probably because John seems like an Enneagram Type 4, like me. I dream of having dinner with John and the prophet Jeremiah at a small bistro table on a street corner in heaven one day. Now, what a party that would be. We'd share some new wine as we talked about the complex things taking shape in our souls. I'm sure there would be a lot of laughter and tears between the three of us. Maybe too many if that's possible on that side of eternity. I knew John would have an impact on our church, but I also had an instant premonition that God would use it in my life as well.

The fall of 2020 was a busy one. Every September, we do an event called Saturated at Eleven22. Joby says the problem with grown-ups is that they quit going to camp. Saturated is the antidote; it's camp for grown-ups. It is four days of intense worship and focused Bible teaching preceded by twenty-one days of fasting in preparation. In many ways, it's the Super Bowl of the calendar year for me, and it requires a lot of sweat equity to pull it off. Knowing that I would need a breather between Saturated and Christmas, I had scheduled a three-day solitude trip to Northern Montana in the late fall. Full disclosure, I have historically not had the foresight for this sort of thing. Ashley graciously agreed to it, and my leaders encouraged me and afforded me the time. Their generosity pushed me over the edge. I booked a round-trip ticket from Jacksonville to Kalispell and found a small Airbnb in Whitefish, which was one right-hand turn and a twenty-minute drive from the airport. It was also about thirty scenic minutes from the southwestern gate of Glacier National Park—God's country.

Now, about fifteen years or so removed from my time traveling with Michael W., I had learned something about myself. During that season, I had a built-in rhythm of finding myself alone with free time in places I had never been before, specifically overseas. I would explore, and it was like fuel to me. I would observe unfamiliar people and places with one half of my brain while thinking big thoughts about God, existence, identity, and purpose with the other. I missed this. It had been a while, as the past ten years had been lived at a breakneck pace. I had been involved in ten multi-site campus launches in very large, rapidly growing churches. I experienced immense pain, transition, and blessing. It had been a good bit of doing. It was time for some *being*. Identity preceding activity is always better than the opposite.

I had an intentionally unstructured approach to the time that I was to spend out there. I packed a camo backpack (something I never thought I'd have) with my Bible, a Thomas Merton book, a set of AirPods, a blue nylon Eno hammock, and a water bottle. I also bought a pair of hiking boots. I've always been a sucker for appropriate footwear. I tried to break them in as much as possible before the trip to avoid blisters. I wanted to travel light and easy on purpose. I felt I could think more clearly and listen more closely with as few distractions as possible. Yet what I wanted more than anything else—what I needed more than anything else—was to be with God. To allow Him to speak, and to put myself in a position where I could hear Him as clearly and as often as possible. As the trip approached, my anticipation for that very thing grew.

The day the plane landed in Kalispell was magical, and the days to come would follow suit—notably warm, cloudless fall days for being that close to the Canadian border. As we touched down, I looked out the window. The afternoon sunlight peaked through the mountains to the east of the runway, making the changing trees come alive. The air was crisp and clean, and the sky was blue and huge. I rented a white Ford F-150 while I was out there.

I guess some Eleven22 had made its way into my veins, birthing the desire to do so. On the way to check into where I would sleep, I pulled the truck into a local grocery store and picked up some fruit, beef jerky, dark chocolate, and a bottle of red wine—the bare necessities.

Before I landed, I was probably about 30,000 feet somewhere over the plains of Nebraska when I had concluded that I was going to read slowly through the book of 1 John during my time out there. I guess there were a couple of reasons that prompted me in that direction. It was short, for one. I wanted to take my time and read it slowly. But more than that, I wanted it to read *me* deeply. (Again, I love John.) Also, I figured this would be a good way to till the soil of my heart in preparation for what was to come during the year of relationships, not for the sake of work, but to allow the Spirit of God to work in me. I was looking forward to the time that we would spend diving into the heart and mind of the disciple whom Jesus loved. For those reasons and a few others, it was settled.

I woke up the next morning at 5:00 am, packed my backpack with the necessities for the day, and headed toward the entrance to Glacier National Park. It was still pitch black when I arrived. After passing through the entrance, I made my way along the south side of Lake McDonald on Going-To-The-Sun Road by faith and headlight. I had a sense that I was surrounded by a good bit of natural beauty, but I couldn't see much in the dark. There were no streetlights there, and no cell service either. But there were a lot of stars—thousands of them. It took a lot of discipline to keep my eyes on the road with what was available to be seen directly overhead.

I pulled into a parking lot at the Avalanche Creek trailhead a few miles into the park and waited for the night sky to give way to some daylight. The silence in the truck was deafening. When dawn started to break, I climbed out of the truck, found the map at the trailhead, and started the hike to Avalanche Lake alone and in the quiet. The morning air was brisk enough for me to see my breath as I walked. You don't get that sort of thing in Florida very often. It was a needed change of pace. Glacier is otherworldly as it wakes up every morning. It's like a cathedral that demands reverence and reflection. Around every corner, there were blessings to greet me. Evidence of God, both small and grandiose in scale. Grace in the subtle movement of the rocky stream flowing at my feet. Grandeur in morning light hitting the jagged mountain peaks overhead. Glory in the opportunity to take it all in silence and solitude. It was awe-inspiring.

I had sung many songs of worship and adoration in front of many people in the years that had gone by. All right, good, and true. Now, in this moment, God was allowing me the opportunity for my soul to catch up with the words that I had sung. The trail became a *beth-el*, a place of worship for me—God's house. For those not familiar, that's the place where Jacob the liar had his dream of the ladder extending between heaven and earth. It wouldn't take much for me to convince myself that I have some Jacob in me. I think we all do. If we deny it, we're probably in deeper trouble than if we flat out admit it. I had undoubtedly been running from some things. Some of those things were outside of me, and some of them were between my own ears. Things that I couldn't realistically escape even if I tried. But God found me there. I mean, I didn't put my head on a rock, although some impressive ones were lying around. But as I walked, the Spirit of Jesus was continually gifting me with a serene sense of His goodness. Like angels ascending and descending on a ladder, my heart was connected to His. This is where real life is lived. Step by step with God, enjoying His company.

Praise God for those moments. I needed that one. I kept putting one boot in front of the other, enjoying each turn in the path until I arrived at the clearing that opened up to the end of the trail to Avalanche Lake. It was a sight to behold. Towering mountain peaks on three sides, each with a strand like a waterfall plummeting thousands of feet to their respective mountains' base. The scale was hard to judge. The falls were so distant I had to squint to see them. They were too far away to be audible, but I'm sure I would be overwhelmed by their immense force should I have taken the initiative to go closer.

In the foreground of my view was a glassy lake of glacier-born water. The surface of the water was protected from the wind by the immense mountains that stood guard around it. The early October trees that dotted the mountains reflected a brilliant display of yellows and oranges off the smooth surface. It looked like a Bob Ross painting. I spent the better part of an hour standing still on the water's edge, trying to take it all in. As I did, I felt small, yet not insignificant, as if I had been given a gift.

God-given gifts like that have a way of allowing you to see His glory and your value simultaneously. These two things would seem contradictory or unable to coexist.

After his disobedience, Adam hid from God. He was dismissed from His presence in his shame. But somehow by God's grace, through His cross, under the shadow of His covering, I was with Him. In this gift, I saw my true identity in who God had created me to be. His gracious demeanor stood in stark contrast to the cutting words that had dug at the foundations of my God given identity. He was reminding me that I was made in His image, to reflect His nature as purely as the trees reflected in the still water before me. I had been a mess. My anger and resentment had created waves in my soul that distorted His character in me. At that moment, God was calming me down. Speaking "peace be still" to the storm in my heart and shielding me from the wind like the tall mountains that surrounded the lake. He was behind me and before me. A strong tower to run to for safety.

By His grace, my heart and mind began to come to terms with where I was and who I was. He was perfecting His image in me. I walked along the water's edge and found two healthy pine tree trunks about fifteen feet apart. I dug through my backpack for the Eno hammock and set it up. After entrusting my weight to it, I grabbed my Bible. Having been led through one of the most meaningful worship services I had experienced in a long time by the majesty of my surroundings, I opened to 1 John and let the Word of God speak to me.

> *Beloved, I am writing you no new commandment, but an old commandment that you had from the beginning. The old commandment is the word that you have heard. At the same time, it is a new commandment that I am writing to you, which is true in him and in you, because the darkness is passing away and the true light is already shining. Whoever says he is in the light and hates his brother is still in darkness. Whoever loves his brother abides in the light, and in him there is no cause for stumbling. But whoever hates his brother is in the darkness and walks in the darkness and does not know where he is going, because the darkness has blinded his eyes.*
>
> (1 John 2:7-11)

As I read John's words, the sun began to grow more intense through the pine tree branches over my head. The blue nylon hammock started to glow in response. The air temperature began to shift upward. My ability to see my breath in the morning air disappeared. The detail in the crags and cracks of the mountains that surrounded me began to come into sharp detail as they took in the light. Things internal and external began to come into focus. I had no premeditated plans on that hike to think about Ben, about Phoenix, about all that had transpired years before. I certainly had no plans to consider what had transpired in our home during my middle school years. Yet I knew I had taken them with me. They were hiding in the dark shadows of my heart. But something was happening. I had a keen awareness that I was being offered an invitation.

A gracious command. He knew what needed to happen within me, and like a good Shepherd, He was leading me to it.

Just a few years prior, I had picked up a rock on the shore of the Sea of Galilee and hurled it into the water. I was begrudgingly obedient. At that point, I did what I needed to do. But here, on the shore of this mountain lake, something different was happening. I felt a thing drop from my head to my gut. Like the end of a branch that's connected to a vine, the Spirit of Jesus was birthing something that I was incapable of creating on my own. He was lovingly commanding me to do something He has lovingly commanded many to do in the past and will continue to command many more to do in the future—to "follow me." It wasn't audible, but it was undeniable. Not only was He issuing the command, but He was also giving me the power to take Him up on it.

In all honesty, there is no way that I would have had any natural proclivity toward trading in my heavy burden of anger for his light yoke of grace. But this invitation to leave the shadows and to journey in step with Jesus into the light was something I couldn't pass up. The weight of it made the prospect of holding on to my anger and hurt seem so small. There in that hammock on the side of Avalanche Lake, a miracle happened. My perspective shifted. I forgave Ben. Not because I had convinced myself that he was forgivable, but because the adventure of following Jesus was far more attractive. I had never seen things like this before. I had been living in the desert of duty-based obedience. I was living under the crushing weight of obligation. I was missing the point. John's words were inviting me into the delight of proximity to the Master. They were summoning me back into the garden of his kindness to walk with Him in the cool of the day. These two things couldn't be more different. One will eventually kill you. The other will well up in you like a spring of Living Water.

The following two days consisted of me wandering through Montana's natural beauty with a lighter heart than I had experienced in years. I saw every sunrise and every sunset. I lay on the hood of the F-150 at a lookout point on the side of Going-To-The-Sun Road, which looked over the deep river valley, and watched the stars pop out one by one as the sun disappeared behind the mountains. They overwhelmed me. I finished 1 John. It overwhelmed me, too.

When I got home, there was a marked difference in my demeanor. Ashley noticed it. I was more prone to smile. More prone to cry when the situation called for it. More prone to notice the good gifts around me, and as a result, more prone to have gratitude for them. I knew something significant had happened. But I also knew there were some steps to take as a result. Those kinds of God given gifts often lead to further obedience. A few days later, I grabbed my phone, pulled up a number I hadn't dialed in a long time, and pressed the green button. My heart raced a little bit as the phone rang, but it calmed down when he picked up on the other side.

"Hey Ben," I said. "Hey, Michael," Ben responded. I tried to tell him what had happened. I told him about my trip to Montana. I shared about 1 John. I'm not sure the particular words I used made sense in the order that I used them, but I had the sense that he knew what was happening. I think we had both been waiting for it. Something had to give, and it was. I began to explain the purpose of my call further. “My pastor, Joby, said that 2021 would be the year of relationships,” I mentioned. “I think what’s happening with me has something to do with it. We’re going to spend twenty-four weeks in the book of John together as a church, discovering how to love each other in light of who Jesus is. I want to write a bunch of songs about it, too. I miss doing that with you. I miss it a lot. I would love it if you would be a part of it in some way.”

We weren’t in the same room. We weren’t even in the same state, but I could tell that both our hearts were getting warmer as we discussed the possibility. He said he would be honored to be included, which meant a lot. I knew his time had become more valuable as the years passed, with his growing family and increased responsibilities at the church in Phoenix. He was one of the executive pastors. It was a demanding role. I floated the idea of flying him in for a songwriter’s retreat that I was planning for our team in the early spring. We would spend two or so days focused on a few key passages in John and see what God would give us creatively out of it. We agreed it was a good place to start. The dates and details were settled. As I pushed purchase on the flights, I remembered throwing the rock.

CHAPTER 10

Through a series of unusual circumstances, Eleven22 had acquired a property known as Cabin Bluff just across the Florida-Georgia line from Jacksonville. The land had a storied history dating all the way back to the time of the Timucua, a tribe of Native Americans who populated the region before it was settled. Cabin Bluff was founded in the 1920s by industrialist Howard Coffin and was commonly recognized as the oldest hunt club in the United States. Calvin Coolidge, who was a friend of Coffin's, had used it as his presidential retreat; it was his Camp David. It's a beautiful plot of land situated on the banks of the Cumberland River just off the Atlantic coast. Dense Georgia Pine forests and ready access to the open water made it an outdoorsman's dream.

The church transformed Cabin Bluff into an Eleven22 retreat center to foster and deepen relationships among attendees. There was something magical about the place. Particularly, the majestic oak hammocks laced with Spanish moss that framed the eastward view out over the river from the main lodge. It made for some magical sunrises. There was also a large cast-iron fire pit with eight old Adirondack chairs surrounding it, in view of the riverbank. The number of stories that had been shared around that circle over the years would be hard to measure. I would be hard-pressed to think of a more idyllic setting for writing songs, or anything else, for that matter. The leadership of the church was kind enough to let us use it for the songwriter's retreat. And, as God's sovereign hand would have it, we were able to schedule it so the Shanes could be a part of it. They would lead worship at our Thursday night and Sunday morning services, and in the days between join us for the retreat. I mentioned the idea of hunting at the retreat center to E, and he perked up at the prospect. I knew we wouldn't see him very much during our time there. I also mentioned that Ben would be joining us. B said, "Ben is gonna be there?! This will be like church camp." He waited a moment and then said, "Hey, can I borrow a guitar?" I knew exactly what guitar he wanted.

As it turned out, both the Shanes and Ben arrived on the same day. I drove to the airport to pick up Ben. We would drive directly to Eleven22 so I could meet the Shanes at sound check for the Thursday night service. I knew what we were about to do was the right thing, but I still had some butterflies in my stomach about it. This was a big deal. There were a lot of emotions and thoughts to work through. The anxiety was eased by the fact that Ben's flight was delayed getting from the runway to the gate due to a massive lightning storm and a tornado moving through the immediate area. He was stuck out on the tarmac waiting it out. It doesn't seem like it should have, but it lightened the mood.

We shared some witty text banter. He from his seat on the plane, and me from the driver's seat of my car several hundred yards away. "Make a run for the gate, man, . . . you're too close to turn back now." I chuckled as I looked down at my phone for his response. "This is wild." It was a good start. After half an hour, I recognized his frame as he walked out of the baggage claim doors. He raised his hand, and I opened my car door. We hugged each other. His hair had silvered out. I had more lines on my face. We had both been through a good bit of life since we had last seen each other and, by God's grace, had lived to tell the tale.

The tarmac delay had put me behind schedule in joining the Shanes for the sound check back at church. Ben and I caught up as much as we could while we fought the traffic and weather on our way. There was an odd, unfamiliar feeling pointing out the geography of Jacksonville to him as we drove. For so much of our lives, we had experienced things together: college, marriage, Michael W., kids, and Phoenix. Now he was living in the desert, and I was living in the tropics. Everything that we saw through the windows represented the life I had lived after the traumatic departure. He had never driven over the Dames Point bridge. He didn't know about Eleven22. He had never met Joby. We had spent five years apart, curating new experiences and relationships. At the same time, we were both aware

friend. Brody poked his head out from around the corner. He was substantially taller than the last time Ben had seen him. "Brody, do you remember Uncle Ben?" I asked. He silently nodded his head as we all doted on how much he had grown. He shyly sauntered up to bed when he couldn't take it anymore. Ben was disappointed that the other two were already down for the night. It had been such a long time. Beckett was just a few months old when we left Arizona. There was a lot to catch up on, but we didn't have the time to do it. Even if we tried, we wouldn't scratch the surface. Ashley made Ben promise to give Jen, Anna, and Liam our love as we made our way to the car. He assured her that he would.

When we arrived at the retreat center, the fire had already been lit, and the conversations had begun. Most of our worship staff had made the journey up from where they had led at their respective campuses that night. Both Shanes were there. Joby even came up to join us for the evening. There were about fifteen of us in total. It was a collision of worlds. I sat back and observed everybody as they engaged in conversation. There were a lot of smiles in the firelight, and the sound of laughter was more common than not. There was a blessing in it.

At one point, I looked up and through the flicker of the flames I noticed Ben and Joby settling into a conversation. Joby knew who this guy was and the part that he had played in my landing at Eleven22. "Surreal," I thought as I leaned back in the Adirondack chair. I never thought that I would see those two enjoying each other's company. But it was happening right in front of my eyes. You can't tell me God doesn't have a sense of humor. The cast-iron fire pit was working its magic on all of us, drawing out funny stories from years gone by. We settled into a rhythm of listening when someone would lead out with, "Man, this one time . . ." It was striking how much common history Ben and I had to pull from. Between the Shanes, Ben, and me, we could have held court well into the morning. As the fire died down, the numbers started to dwindle. We stayed up a little longer, catching up on things that had happened over the last five years. I put my head on my pillow that night with a deep sense of satisfaction for how the time was spent.

After breakfast the next morning, we made the turn to focus on what we had come there to accomplish. To start, we all sat around the table in Coolidge Tavern on the south end of the property. I opened my Bible to John 13, and the room quieted down as I began to read: "Now before the Feast of the Passover, when Jesus knew that his hour had come to depart out of this world to the Father, having loved his own who were in the world, he loved them to the end" (John 13:1). Jesus, the Master, washed his disciples' dirty, disgusting feet—even Judas Iscariot's, who would betray him minutes later. Peter argued, as usual. Jesus calmed him down. Then he ended by saying:

> *Do you understand what I have done to you? You call me Teacher and Lord, and you are right, for so I am. If I then, your Lord and Teacher, have washed your feet, you also ought to wash one another's feet. For I have given you an example, that you also should*

do just as I have done to you. Truly, truly, I say to you, a servant is not greater than his master, nor is a messenger greater than the one who sent him. If you know these things, blessed are you if you do them.
(John 13:12-17)

I told the team about what Ben and I had been through as we sat across the table from one another. Not all of it, but most of it. I looked at him as I tried to describe how sad the loss of our friendship had made us. His eyes let everyone know that he agreed. I told them how angry I had been. How confused we had both been. I told them about Galilee, Montana, and 1 John, and the invitation that Jesus offered me to follow. I told them about the phone call inviting Ben to the table where we now sat. Then I said to them that after years of pain, I was ready to admit that I loved my brother no matter what. That taking Jesus up on that invitation was more valuable than holding on to my anger and unforgiving heart.

Ben spoke as well. We both worked through it together right there in front of everybody. It was honest and raw, but ultimately redemptive. I know people tend to lean toward living in measurable realities. In general, we believe that if something can be quantified, its value can be understood. I realize how that sort of thinking applies to things that exist in the material world: money, market trends, comparable data, etc. That's helpful stuff. But there is an unquantifiable value in confession. You can't assign a metric to it. It's a spiritual thing. When it happens, when you reach that place where the layers between your projected, protected self-image and your actual self disappear, you are known for who you really are. Things shift.

Inspired by what we had just shared, the team broke up into small groups and scattered around the property to start the songwriting process. I had planned that Ben, the Shanes, and I would be together. E would pop in and out as he felt he was helpful, especially knowing that there was game to hunt and fish to catch nearby. We all headed to the main lodge, each with a guitar in hand. B inevitably gravitated toward the Gibson. Ben had a beautiful spruce top McPherson that I had been given as a gift by the guy who made it. That guitar is an absolute work of art. I had a Martin D-28, a workhorse of a guitar, punchy and bright. It is perfect for Bluegrass or Americana. All incredible instruments in their own right, but the Gibson had tenure. It was the mature older brother of the bunch and had the bruises to prove it. We walked through the front door of the main lodge and made ourselves comfortable.

The main lodge is one of the oldest structures on the property, oozing with classic hunt club charm. It's a one-story bungalow situated just off the banks of the Cumberland River. It had been painted a deep olive green so as not to stand out from its surroundings. Its open vaulted ceiling and exposed wood beams supported two huge antique wagon wheel chandeliers overhead. There are two opposing stone fireplaces, each with impressive hearths on the north and south walls. Upon acquiring the property, the church had decided to retain everything in it as it was when it was the historic Hunt Club. As a result, the living area of the main lodge is a legit outdoorsman's trophy room. The paneled walls are covered with taxidermy that had been harvested from the property throughout its over a hundred years of existence, along with old black-and-white photos of past patrons who had visited. I have no idea what Calvin Coolidge looks like, but he's probably featured in one of them. There are bobcats, turkeys, rattlesnakes, and multiple whitetail deer heads situated strategically around the main living room. There's even an imposing twelve-foot alligator with its jaws wide open mounted to the ceiling over the front door. The east end of the lodge features double doors that open onto a covered porch overlooking the river. If you had to pick a place to be creative, this was a good one. And, for me, if you had to pick a group of guys to write a song with, these were the guys.

I often get asked questions about the process of writing songs. "What comes first, lyrics or music?" Or "How do you come up with a good melody?" My answer to those questions is that there is no process. There's just a wrestling match with your heart and your mind, and in this case, John 13. However, in this particular wrestling match, I was excited about what each contributor would bring to the mat.

B is a tenacious songwriter. He is rarely willing to give in until he feels a thing is fully fleshed out, and even after, his wheels are spinning. It was great to see Ben with a guitar in his hands again. It brought a buoyancy to my spirit and a smile to my face. For the next few hours, we gave ourselves permission to create in front of each other without fear of criticism.

Songs, when they are finished, can be beautiful. However, there is often a beauty that precedes the finished product, and that is the grace shared between the contributors along the way. Melodies are meddled with, chord progressions are constructed, and words are pieced together out of thin air. It's like an artist mixing colors on a palette, trying to evoke what is in their heart in visible form on a blank canvas. As we tussled through the process, things began to take shape. In two verses, a chorus, and a bridge, we had taken on the impossible task of trying to convey the depth of Jesus's unconditional love, experienced by the disciples, as He washed their feet. It felt like trying to pour the Atlantic Ocean into a Dixie cup. The crazy thing is that we were experiencing that same love as we worked together. A lot was happening at once. In the tussle, something began to take shape.

Man of sorrows
Cast down with grief
Despised, afflicted
For all to see
The Lamb of God was slain
Now I am free
I give my life to love
As you've loved me

How deep the Father's love for us
How vast that crimson sea
I give my life, Lord Jesus
To love as You first loved me

Our hearts lit up as the three of us belted it out together. The sound of our voices resonated inside the old wooden room. E meandered in and nodded his head in approval as it went down. Again, there is an inherent beauty when brothers unify like that. Some might call it *anointed*, smooth as oil gushing over the head and down the beard of God's chosen man.

The wrestling match wore us out. We had expended a lot of heart, soul, mind, and strength, and we needed a break. We felt good about what we had uncovered, so we got up. I put the D-28 in its case. Ben carefully propped the McPherson on the old leather couch where he had been sitting. B held on to the Gibson. He couldn't bring himself to put it down. Honestly, it suited him. We walked out the double doors onto the porch, which overlooked the river, to get a change of scenery and some fresh air.

Now, as previously stated, when the church acquired Cabin Bluff, the decision was made to leave everything as is. This included the furniture out on the porch. There were four wooden Adirondack chairs, a small outdoor couch with a coffee table in front of it, and a side table that ran parallel to the exterior wall of the bungalow. On that table, there was a molded cement ashtray in the shape of a man's hand. It was sculpted palm up as if to catch the ashes of the cigars being smoked by the hunters who had sat on that porch recounting their adventures over the last century. Whereas an average, every day, ordinary type of person wouldn't notice an ashtray like that and pass over it without thinking twice, B and E saw it as an opportunity. After all, E *is* geared toward global domination.

Who knows what all transpires in the minds of people to make them do the things they do? There could have been a residual buzz in B's mind from the song that we had just written, for all I know. Or it could be that they just live their lives in a constant state of proactive, outside-the-box creativity—like, *all* the time. They have numerous ideas and a large audience that enjoys hearing them. Rightly so. In either case, the opportunity was seized.

Immediately, B turned into a Hollywood film director, and we all instinctively knew how to help him bring his artistic vision to life. He instructed E to pick up the hand and pull his sleeve down over his wrist to create the illusion that it was a prosthetic. It was comically unconvincing. Without being asked, Ben grabbed his phone out of his pocket and positioned himself to capture what was about to happen. I stood behind Ben and watched with a grin on my face. B pulled his phone out of his pocket and placed it on the porch floor, screen up, and hinted at pointing the headstock of the Gibson downward toward it as if it were a putter unsheathed from a golf bag.

Now, I can't honestly say that I'm familiar with all of Adam Sandler's work. He's had a pretty good run at the box office over the years and reinvented himself a time or two. I can honestly say that his early work is his best. It's common knowledge that there are a few standout moments that have become pillars in modern culture. And here in this moment, with high irony, all the ingredients were there for us to explore one of them. We were all simultaneously overtaken by the spirit of Happy Gilmore himself and were transported to the pivotal putting-green coaching session between him and his one-handed coach, Chubbs. It couldn't have been more obvious what was to be done. So, we did it. Ben pressed the red button to begin the scene. E snapped into character, his eyes intently gazing at his counterpart from under the rim of that hat. As he gently swayed the fake prosthetic ashtray hand, he delivered his line, "Just *tap* it in . . . Just *tap* it in."

Ben and I stood behind the camera, trying not to laugh audibly so we wouldn't ruin the take. B gently lifted his eyes to meet E's as he started slowly swinging the headstock of the Gibson toward his phone in a putting motion in response. "Just *tap* it in. *Tap* it in . . ." And so, he did.

B made the slightest contact. The headstock of the Gibson barely grazed the phone that lay on the porch floor. There was an abrupt *crack!* In the blink of an eye, the headstock burst off the neck of the guitar and began to dangle from the six strings that were now the only thing still holding it on. B stood there in the wake of the moment with the wreckage slung over his shoulder. Horrified, his jaw dropped as he tried to process what had just happened. E recoiled, pulling the ashtray hand to his mouth as if it were his own. From the deepest part of his gut, he grunted, "Michael!" Ben's and my giggles from behind the camera were stunted by audible gasps. Ben's film footage instantly began to take on a Blair Witch Project feel as his steady hand gave way to the moment. It came to a sudden end.

It's been said that the blessing is in the breaking. Now I know that it's true. It's rarely realized in the moment, but it's true. I had been bound by so many heavy burdens. The expectations I had when Ben and I moved to Phoenix that were met with the cutting words of an influential leader who valued organizational progress over pastoral care. The ensuing questions that arose in my soul about my identity as a man when he said what he said. The dearest friendship I had ever experienced that was squeezed to death in the vice of an ugly power struggle. The anxiety that had seized my body and mind like a tyrannical dictator as I tried to lead God's people in song on Easter Sunday morning of 2015. I felt such loss. The deep betrayal from Ben at the coffee shop. The chaos that was unleashed. The friends that disappeared in the rear-view mirror as the rain fell in Phoenix. The lonely tears that Ashley and I had shed on the couch in Jacksonville. I had carried them all around with me like a 500-pound weight strapped to my chest. But God was in it. He was in all of it. He invited me to throw the rock in Galilee. He made my heart quicken as the sun rose over the mountains in Montana. And when that headstock burst off that guitar, He made something beautiful break in me.

I began to laugh. The dam in my soul exploded with immediate, uncontrollable joy. In one passing glance, I saw E with the hand, B with the Gibson's dangling headstock . . . and Ben. It was a God ordained gift. I lit up like an acetylene torch. I couldn't catch my breath as the laughter poured out. There was nothing I could do to stop it. I eventually dropped to my knees and began to roll around on the porch like a toddler. My abs shook as I gasped for air.

No one knew how to take it. I was laughing with such intensity that it began to draw spectators. They left their respective songwriting groups to see what the commotion was about. One bystander mentioned that he thought it sounded like I was calling turkeys. After all, we were at the oldest hunt club in the country. I didn't care; I was lost in the moment. They all stood with bewildered looks on their faces as they saw the fake prosthetic hand, the lame duck guitar in B's hands, and my hysteria.

Common sense would not point to laughter as a reaction. I'm sure some of them started to question my level of sanity, knowing the value of the guitar and how dear it was to me. But there's no way that they could understand all of what God was accomplishing in my heart in that moment. I was drowning in a Spirit-infused catharsis that was years in the making, and it was priceless. It's true that the guitar was valuable, but there was a deeper truth that was bubbling to the surface. Do you know what's more valuable than a '69 Gibson J45? *Brotherhood!* The kind of brotherhood that weathers the deepest of wounds. The kind that can withstand years of pain and come out with its heart beating on the other side because it's rooted in something deeper than imposter "love" for self's sake. It's rooted in genuine *love* for God's sake. The Shanes had lived it out for decades. Ben and I were just discovering it. It's the pure kind of love that lacks nothing and gives everything. The kind of love that's being eternally volleyed back and forth between the three members of the Godhead. It's where you and I came from. It's what we're being invited back to. It's a love that compelled a King to kneel, to take up a basin and towel, and scrape animal waste from His friends' feet. "See what kind of love the Father has given to us, that we should be called children of God; and so we are" (1 John 3:1).

> *Behold, how good and pleasant it is when brothers dwell in unity! It is like the precious oil on the head, running down on the beard, on the beard of Aaron, running down on the collar of his robes! It is like the dew of Hermon, which falls on the mountains of Zion! For there the Lord has commanded the blessing, life forevermore.* (Psalm 133)

From where I sit right now, not much has changed in a practical sense. As I type this, I'm sitting at the same table in the local sandwich shop where Joby first cast the Eleven22 vision to me five years ago. Ben is still in Phoenix. He's one of the executive pastors at CCV. B and E are in Dallas, thinking out of the box and dreaming of global domination. We've enjoyed a healthy amount of group text banter over what we shared together. As far as I know, the Gibson is still in two pieces. E jumped into business mode on it and had it sent to the kind folks at the Gibson Custom Shop in Nashville. If anybody can fix it, they can. We'll see what happens. I'm not worried about it.

Yet I'll tell you what has changed—my heart. I'm not angry. That 500-pound weight that was strapped to my chest is pretty much gone. I now have some time and perspective on all that happened. When I look back on it, my natural inclination is to smile. If that's not a miracle, I don't know what is. Remember, it took years for Joseph to come to the point where he could look at his brothers and honestly say he saw the purpose in the pain. I like to think he smiled when he looked back as well. I think he smiled at his brothers, and at the fact that there were a whole bunch of folks in Egypt and beyond that had food to eat. I don't have a corner on the market of God's wisdom by any stretch of the imagination, but I believe He is working all things out for the good of those who love Him and are called according to His purpose. And in the end, we'll all see the blessing through the brokenness.

GUIDED REFLECTION

It was the late first century. John, the self-proclaimed "disciple whom Jesus loved," had spent decades living in response to the reality of what he had experienced with his friend Jesus of Nazareth, the Messiah. He had been personally recruited by Him as one of the twelve and had been in His presence for the three years of his earthly ministry. He witnessed His arrest and death by Roman crucifixion under the influence of the Jewish hierarchy. And he held face-to-face conversations with Jesus on the other side of an empty tomb. These realities shaped the rest of John's life. So much so that he finds himself in exile on the Greek island of Patmos under the persecution of Emperor Domitian for talking so much about it. There on a Sunday, the same day of the week his friend had come back to life, John is swept away in a trance born of the Spirit of that same Jesus. His mind floods with imagery and color that leaks out through his pen. It is a Revelation.

In one particular scene of his vision, John finds himself walking through an open door into a heavenly throne room. His description of the throne, the One seated upon it, and all that surrounded them is specifically vivid: an enthroned King with the appearance of jasper and carnelian surrounded by the pageantry of uniformly dressed elders, each with a golden crown atop their head. There

were living creatures clad with seeing eyes, singing endless songs of praise, accompanied by a display of heavenly lightning and echoing thunder.

In John's vision, the one seated on the throne held a scroll that was sealed tightly with seven seals. The sealed scroll was generating a palpable tension in the throne room. John felt it. It was as if the destiny of the entirety of John's vision, all of the elders and creatures and the world in which they lived—not to mention John himself— were hanging in the balance of what was written on it. John knew that whatever was on that scroll was what the King intended, and John wanted what the King wanted with everything he was. His desire began to boil up in his belly. Just when he couldn't take it anymore, somebody in the throne room lifted their voice to put words on what he and everybody else were feeling. A mighty angel shouted the question, "Who is worthy to open the scroll and break its seals?" (Revelation 5:2). *Silence.*

John, along with the rest of the characters in his heavenly vision, was overtaken by an immense wave of grief. He knew that both his and the rest of his heavenly companions' sense of peace and purpose depended on what was on the scroll, but it was unattainable. Neither he nor anyone else in that throne room had the authority to break the seals to unleash what the King wanted. John began to sob like a baby. He looked at the King, whose grip around the scroll seemed immovable. He was filled with hopelessness. Then, at the deepest point of his grief, one of the crowned elders looked him in the eye and spoke. "Weep no more; behold, the Lion of the tribe of Judah, the Root of David, has conquered, so that he can open the scroll and its seven seals" (Revelation 5:5).

John felt the atmosphere of the room shift as Jesus, his friend, appeared before the throne. John describes His appearance as that of a Lamb who was standing but appeared as one who had been slain. Meaning, the wounds from his crucifixion hadn't completely disappeared. In fact, they were still very visible, but now they were very different. There was a metamorphosis. The wounds had been transformed into scars, and those scars now played a role in Jesus's unique authority to break the seals and unleash the heart of the enthroned King. The very thing that John was desperate for. The throne room exploded with joy! The creatures and elders, along with a multitude of angels, now revived with a new sense of vitality and hope, burst out in song. It was as if Jesus's healed wounds and authority to break the seals gave them a feeling that a new hope could break out in their own lives.

In the previous guided reflection section of this book, we opened ourselves up to recognizing our own wounds. We discussed the dangers of journeying eastward out of Eden with an unattended bleeding heart and how it can lead us to a heartless kind of living. Maybe you've spent some time digging into your own story and have recognized some things about yourself. Perhaps I've touched on some memories, and it hurts. While this is a necessary part of the restoration journey, there's an inherent danger in doing this sort of thing. You might be tempted to hang out in your own pain. To make it your home. I had been doing this for a long time. In my life, it looked like years of sorrow and anger from betrayal, both from my father and my closest friend. I was drawn to my own pain like flies are drawn to a dead carcass. I knew it wasn't the right place to be, but it fed me. In some ways, it felt like all I knew. That is, until I threw the rock into the Galilee and went on the Montana journey with 1 John.

The reason we spent time reimagining John's apocalyptic Patmos vision together is that it reminds us that in Jesus our wounds can find purpose. This is true for me, and it is true for you. They may hurt like hell, but they are not to be wallowed in any longer than the season that Jesus spent in His borrowed tomb. Jesus's sudden presence in heaven's throne room, scars and all, and His authority to break the seals and unleash the King's intentions meant something to John. He no longer had to wallow in tears. "Weep no more!" The Lamb was about to break the King's redemptive plan wide open, snapping the seals on that scroll like the neck of the '69 Gibson. Euphoric worship and laughter would ensue. Now what was painful had (and has) a sense of destination and purpose. Things are moving in the direction of redemption and reconciliation because of the Lamb's scars. Maybe you've never allowed yourself to believe that your life could be any bigger than your wound. Like me, you've spent a good amount of time stewing in the hurt. What your father, mother, friend, spouse, etc., did to you has become your permanent address.

My prayer is that this time of reflection would challenge you to pick up your own Galilee rock or go on your own Montana journey. I can guarantee you that the same Jesus who inspired John to write his love letter, the one he saw in his Patmos vision, is alive and well and has done everything that needs to be done to ensure your healing. His Spirit is at work in this very moment, accomplishing the renewal that He paid for with His own wounds. Perhaps the call to leave your place of wounding and follow Jesus on the adventure of forgiveness and reconciliation is coming alive in you, just as it did in me. Maybe there's a phone call to make. A debt to cancel. A burden to entrust into His hands. Sounds good, doesn't it? With this Jesus at the helm of your life, who knows what might break open?

PRAYER

Father,

I've recognized my wound.

I've been tempted to allow myself to be defined by it.

I know it's not the right thing to do. Now I'd like to move on.

I want to follow You, but I need help.

There are some things that I've been carrying around that need to be broken off me, but I don't have the power or authority to do it on my own.

There are some people I need to forgive, and there are some painful memories that need to be re-framed in my mind.

I want to see what You want for me fully realized in my life.

I want it more than I want to hold on to my pain.

I believe that Jesus's scars are all that's needed for this to be so.

Jesus, I invite you to break whatever is tying me to my wound so I can follow You fully on the adventure of forgiveness and freedom.

I know I am healed by Your wounds, and I believe that my scars will have purpose.

It's in Your name and authority, I pray.

Amen.

PART 3

THE HEINTZMAN

Let him easter in us,
be a dayspring to the dimness of us,
be a crimson-cresseted east.

Gerard Manley Hopkins

CHAPTER 11

Ashley and I were married in a beautiful, old Dutch Reformed Church in London, Ontario, Canada, on the afternoon of November 7, 2003. The story of how we met is a favorite to tell. She grew up in a vibrant Pentecostal church called London Gospel Temple (LGT to locals), an oddity in southern Ontario. When we tell stories of our childhood, a beautiful semblance rises to the surface. We were simultaneously spending inordinate amounts of time in charismatically charged worship environments in different countries, completely unbeknownst to each other. When she talks about her childhood church experiences, humor is the pervasive theme. She comes by it honestly by way of her dad, Rick Greven (also known as the venerable "Mr. Fun"). I am grateful for, and indebted to, their lightness of heart. It's a providential balance to my proclivity toward the deep. At times, the stories she tells are eerily reminiscent of my boyhood antics with Jimmy Nichols. LGT was known for being a church that worshipped God, specifically, for how their music spurred it on. This brings us to the common denominator between Ashley and me: Dave Pedde, the music pastor at LGT during Ashley's childhood. Dave created the worship music that shaped my wife's upbringing, much like my dad created the music that shaped me. Dad from the organ bench; Dave from the piano. My mother-in-law, Gayle Greven ("Double G"), is known to recount stories of Dave underscoring Sunday night prayer services that extended well past their allotted time as he tarried at the altar in God's presence. Dave was (and still is) a great worship leader. The thing is, he can do it without singing. When Dave sits in front of the piano keys, the worship of God pours out of him. And it spills out on whoever happens to be around him at the time. I experienced this in my college years. After years of investing in the community at LGT, Dave decided to jump into the academic world. He and his family moved to the States, where he took a teaching job at North Central Bible College. He would spend some of the most productive years of his life investing in young people who were training for full-time music ministry. I was one of them, and so was Ben. Come to think of it, so was Jimmy Nichols.

I met Dave when I arrived as a freshman at North Central in the fall of 1997. Dave was my piano teacher. He was also my pastor, my therapist, and my friend. We would often neglect major and minor scales as well as Ionian and Dorian modes, for deep dives into the issues of the heart. I found in Dave a trusted confidant who was committed to seeing me develop into mature manhood in Christ, something I desperately needed at that time in my life. To this day, he's the only person whom I've ever referred to as a mentor. His influence even breaks through my disdain for corporate leadership teams. That's a big deal.

Dave was a frustrated songwriter. It takes one to know one. In fact, I've rarely met one who wasn't. Toward the end of our college days, Ben and I, along with a few others, helped Dave make a singer/songwriter record to scratch his creative itch. We were honored to be a part of it. The summer after it was finished, Dave, his oldest son Devin, Ben, and I got in his minivan and traveled through the Midwest playing his music in Assemblies of God churches along the way. We left Minneapolis and made our way through successive states, staying in homes where we could keep costs down. We hugged Interstate 94 down through Wisconsin into the Chicagoland area, staying in the St. Charles house. We made the turn around the lake toward Ben's hometown of Kalamazoo, Michigan, before crossing the border into Ontario, Canada.

We ended up in London, Dave's old stomping ground, playing a Sunday night concert at his closest friend's church, who just happened to be Ashley's pastor. That's where Ashley and I met; it was love at first sight. When it happened, she was nearly engaged to someone else. But it was epically undeniable. Storybook stuff. It was two eras of Dave's life and ministry colliding. He couldn't believe it. We dated long-distance for about six months. Long-distance relationships have a way of accelerating things. You tend to ask the big questions more quickly. We asked them and got our answers. In fact, Ashley and I saw each other a grand total of ten times before we were at the altar. Dave did our premarital counseling, and he and his best friend (Ashley's pastor) co-officiated our wedding. There's no way that either of us could picture living life without the other. At twenty years and three kids in, we still can't.

The evening before our wedding is still one of the most memorable nights of my life. My in-laws owned an old historic farmhouse on the outskirts of London, Ontario, at 1499 Westdel Bourne. It was built in the early 1800s, pre-electricity. The house oozed character and charm. It was constructed from a unique yellow brick created onsite from the dirt of the sizeable plot of land on which it sat. The acreage provided a sense of solitude from the hustle and bustle of everyday life. It had a large porch wrapping around the back of the house that looked over the property. The view pushed toward the horizon with nothing to stop it. Beyond the property line was a local farmer's field, and beyond that a horse pasture. It was idyllic, and it had a sense of sanctuary to it. It was quiet, safe, and stable. Much of that sense of safety came from the joy that existed in the way Ashley's family related to one another. The way they loved one another. I soaked it in like a dry sponge. The house had been added onto over the years. It had a large attached formal dining and living room that ran the entire length of the house on one side. It was a beautiful room with wood floors and a fireplace.

My father-in-law, Mr. Fun, is Dutch and one of the most fastidious house painters I have ever known. In the years that followed, he would paint the walls of the various homes our family lived in. I remember him making sure that the slots in the tiny white screws that secured the outlet faceplates were all positioned perfectly at high noon. It was a very Dutch thing to do. If something is to be done, it's to be done right. His color of choice for this room was a rich merlot, making it a warm respite in the cold Canadian winters. As we considered the options, it was mutually agreed that this room would be the ideal place for hosting our rehearsal dinner.

We cleared out all the furniture and outfitted the room with tables of various sizes and shapes, each primped to the nines with tablecloth, candle, and décor. The day before our wedding, our closest friends and family descended upon London, Ontario, in preparation for the ceremony. After the short rehearsal, they poured into the house in a frenzy of laughter and excitement. They were greeted with the wonderful warmth of the environment my in-laws had created. The old-world allure of the house worked its magic. There was fire and candlelight, music and wine, and the smell of the delicious food that an old family friend had catered for the event.

We all crammed together in the red room in our assigned seats. All folks from both sides were there. My mom and dad were still married at the time but were already deep in the mire of darkness and depression. They did a good job keeping it to themselves. I'm sure the wedding was a welcome distraction for them, but I felt the tension. I asked my brother to fulfill best man duties and was honored when he accepted. My sister stood up on Ashley's side. Likewise, I asked Ashley's brother-in-law to join mine. Both our lives were intermingling. Mr. Fun and Double G were beside themselves with elation. What more could one ask for than a home filled with the warmth and laughter of intimate relationships on the eve of their only daughter's wedding? They had invested so much in creating a sense of safe harbor, and they had invested so much in Ashley. They were entering the golden years, experiencing the fruit of it all.

Two things occurred to everybody that night. The first was that Dave Pedde was the common thread between all of us from different families, different churches, and even different countries. We were the spokes in the wheel, and he was the hub. When the realization hit him, Dave piped up from his table and emphatically stated, "I'm just realizing that I'm the reason you're all here!" The room exploded with laughter and admiration. We couldn't deny it. The second was that most of the people there were musicians, and very accomplished ones at that. We had pianists, guitar players, a church organist, worship leaders, singers, songwriters, and choir members. We even had a violinist. It should have come as no surprise given Ashley's and my journey, but it snuck up on us that night. We all spoke a similar language. One more nuanced and dynamic than English (or even French). The vast majority of us were fluent in the language of the heart, expressing itself in melody and in harmony, in rhythm and in rhyme. Not only that, but we had all come about discovering this language in God's house. It's the place where we started developing our vocabulary, where we began forming sentences and having conversations. People who speak this language tend to be wired in a certain way. They have an elevated awareness of their emotions at any given moment. They also know how to read a room and improvise accordingly. Both things were at play that night.

In the back of the room that night was an old piano: the Heintzman. It was perched on the back wall of the red room, centered underneath a skylight window. At the start of the night, the piano was an unassuming piece of furniture. During the daytime, light would stream down through the window above, highlighting the old piano against the red wall. It was a visual anchor piece for the room. By the time the party had started, we were well into the evening. Daylight becomes scarcer as fall gives way to winter in Canada. The beautifully adorned tables and candlelight obscured the Heintzman's presence in the room. It was there; we just didn't realize it. But it didn't stay that way.

As we pushed past dinner, the state of the tables began to evolve from crisp and clean to the best kind of messy. The room began to feel lived in. Ashley and I held hands as we took it all in. Napkins were strewn about. There were half-eaten plates of chocolate cake here and there, and glasses of red wine. Conversation over dinner had been civilized and proper. Now that it was over, things were shifting into a new gear. The ability of our guests to simultaneously feel deeply and improvise accordingly began to play out. Pockets of boisterous laughter began to break out. The overall decibel level in the room began to rise dramatically. I squeezed Ashley's hand as I looked around at the smiles, overwhelmed with a sense of gratitude.

I noticed Nathan, my college roommate, get up from his assigned seat. Nathan was a piano performance major at North Central. He was brilliant. But he was more Mozart, and I was more Michael W. Smith. During our college days, I would commonly find him reading old dusty books on the finer points of developing proper technique. He would spend hours in the practice room with old dead composers like Rachmaninoff and Debussy delving into their minds and fleshing out their compositions while the rest of us struggled to read simple chord charts. I would get mad at him and say things like, "Nathan, isn't this a waste of time? You know, somebody at some point had to write these songs you're spending so much time learning. Why don't you just write your own?" It never swayed him much. We were different, but we had a lot of fun. And truth be told, he got me through music theory. For all his academic intensity, Nathan possessed an incredibly sharp sense of wit. He was Canadian and hilarious, in the vein of Mike Meyers, Martin Short, and Leslie Nielsen. It was in his blood.

Unannounced, Nathan snaked through the tables and chairs toward the bench in front of the piano. He sat down, cracked his knuckles out in front of his long torso, and careened all his classical technique into the black and white keys in front of him. What was his repertoire for the evening? The theme song from The Flintstones. The room erupted in unified song. "You'll have a yabba dabba do time, you'll have a do time, you'll have a gay old time!" Everyone shouted "Wilma!" at the top of their lungs.

that we had decades of inside jokes to revisit. And we did. It was wonderful.

Upon arrival, I quickly gave Ben the lay of the land at church. I showed him the studio we had built and introduced him to the members of the staff. Many of them knew he was coming and were aware of what had happened between us. He was gracious as he met each one. I was proud to introduce him as my friend. We eventually made our way into the worship center, where the B and E had already started with the band. It sounded great. They were split-center on the stage. B had the Gibson slung over his right shoulder. He loved that thing. I left Ben at the mix console and snuck up to sit behind the keys.

Thursday is my favorite service of the week. The people come eager to express themselves in worship, and Joby is chomping at the bit to deliver what God had laid on him in the tree stand, where he writes his sermons at the beginning of the week. I loved sharing it with Ben, and I think it was good for him to see it. This is where God had allowed my family and me to land after all that we had been through. I was at peace with what was happening at Eleven22, and he had seen me wrestling for years while we worked together in Phoenix. Ben chuckled at Joby's jokes during the sermon and took note of some points that struck his heart. There was a sense of full circle as we sat next to each other in the seats that night. It was good.

After church, Ben and I snuck back home so he could see where we lived before we headed up to the retreat center to join the rest of the team. I led him through the front door, and Ashley greeted him with the warm embrace of an old

Chapter 11

The lid had been taken off. All the individual pockets of laughter across the room had melded into one giant explosion of joy. It was electric. As a result of Nathan's bold move, the attention naturally shifted to the Heintzman. Having done his part, he promptly vacated the bench, leaving us all expectant for what would happen next. There was no script, no order of events. Whatever would happen next would be pure spontaneity, born out of the context of a deep, common love formed through long-standing relationships.

For some reason, I felt a general sense that whatever was to happen next needed to be championed by the hub of the wheel. He had already disclosed that he was the reason we were all there. After the laughter died down, I made eyes with Dave across the room. The table where Ashley and I were sitting was close enough to the piano for me to be able to touch the bench. I reached out and knocked on it with a closed fist, summoning Dave to lead us. He couldn't turn the groom down. In his gentle, unassuming way, he got up and sauntered toward the Heintzman and sat down. As he did, the room settled with a hush.

We serve a very intentional God. With Him, there are no accidents or mistakes. He knew we needed warmth and light, so He created the sun for His glory and our good. It blazes in the heavens as an unmistakable marker of His greatness. He hung the stars in the sky by the trillions so he could point them out to Abraham and say, "Try and count them." He still hasn't stopped making them. He made birds to fly and fish to swim. When each is in its element, it just works, and everybody knows it.

We all knew what God had created Dave to do. It's not that he's not a funny person. He had a streak of Canadian wit in him all his own. But there was zero percent chance that a television theme song was coming out of him at that moment. As he hunched over the keys, he began to speak his native language—worship. He played a song that he had written years before. We all recognized it. Dave was (and still is) a very humble creature. So much so that I've often thought there was something wrong with him. Not so. He just didn't think of himself very much. He spent his time and energy investing in other people, mostly college students. I'm sure at some point he had dreams of writing chart toppers and radio hits rolling around in the back of his mind. The kind of songs that everybody knows. Things never really played out like that. But on that night, with that particular group of people, it was a different story. We all sang the chorus of Dave's song, "His Great Love," together: "This one thing I'm sure of. This is it: *God is love*. Not that we loved Him, yet He gave His Son. I am convinced of it. It's written that nothing shall ever separate us from His love."

The air in the room shifted. Dave was like the woman who snuck into the dinner party uninvited and dumped priceless perfume on Jesus's feet. We were all caught up in the beautiful aroma emanating from Dave's heart at the piano bench. Each one lent their voice to the sound in beautiful harmony. The sound reverberated off the old wooden floors in the red room. We thought we were at a rehearsal dinner; it turns out we were at a worship service. It was complete with bread and wine, and, on more levels than one, a bride and *bridegroom*. We all recognized the presence of Jesus there that night. He was belly laughing beside us at the table. Each of us took Him in with bread and wine as we enjoyed each other's company. He was kneeling in front of us with a basin and a towel, washing us and showing us how to love and serve one another in an intimate relationship. And He was manifest as we celebrated the purity of his loving heart in song. It wasn't intentional, but it was borderline liturgical.

CHAPTER 12

My wife and I loved visiting Westdel Bourne in the early years of our married life. I would always say, "I would buy this place if I had any money." The black Ontario dirt was wealthier than we were. In the summertime, it was an escape from Nashville's sultry heat. Summers up there are short, but magical. The locals squeeze every second out of them that they possibly can, knowing that winter is just around the corner. For us, the holidays were even better. I would often fly directly up to Detroit from wherever the last Michael W. Christmas show was and spend Christmas with Ashley's family. My wife would pick me up at the airport, and we'd make the two-hour drive up the 401 to London together, catching up on the events of home and the road along the way. I loved holding her hand in the car as we made our way back into her native country. There was a part of her that came alive as we crossed the border.

A subtle smile would creep across her face, knowing that time with her parents was at hand. There are no billboards on the sides of the highways up there—just farmland, windmills, and road signs in French. I could feel the rigors of the touring schedule shake off as we drove into the Ontario countryside. The knowledge that I would be in the same city for a few weeks and that Ashley would be there with me was welcomed.

Every once in a while, I would walk through the old kitchen into the red room and find myself in front of the Heintzman. As I sat down, memories of our worship service rehearsal dinner would flood back into my mind. Gratitude welled up in my heart as the sound of the piano echoed through the old house. I found myself at rest in the realization of all that God had provided for me. I wasn't ignoring the hard stuff, the pain of the animosity between my mom and dad. But I was aware of God's faithfulness through it. I was thankful for the way that He had provided for me along the way. For Northwest, for Jimmy Nichols, for Ben, for Dave Pedde, for Michael W., and now for Ashley, Mr. Fun and Double G. For this whole new dimension of belonging that I was discovering as a part of her family. I was learning a deeper way of loving and being loved and of knowing and being known. For the first time in my life, I had a line of sight on legacy. I could see it in the way that my father-in-law loved his family. In the sense of security and faithfulness he built around Gayle, Ashley, and her brother. I knew that's where I was headed. Brody, Bentley, and Beckett were years from their first breath, but the foundations for the home they would be raised in were being laid.

The Heintzman was somewhere around 100 years old. It had been in Ashley's family for the entirety of its life. It was passed down by Ashley's great-grandfather, Goldy Reid. He bought it for Ashley's great-uncle Jack in the hope that he would learn how to play. Apparently, it didn't take. Goldy decided that its best use was in the house where Ashley's mom was raised, on the Thames River in Chatham, Ontario. Gayle was ten when it arrived. She immediately gravitated toward it, learning the craft. Before long, the house on the river was filled with the sound of the old gospel songs that she had grown up on. There is a legend that the piano survived a house fire in the dead of winter, a few years after it arrived. It was stored in the garage while her dad restored the house. Twelve-year-old Gayle would don her winter coat and head into the garage to brave the subarctic temperatures to play it. Her breath vaporized in the frigid air as her fingers moved about the keys. The Heintzman stayed with her throughout the course of her life until it eventually landed in the red room at Westdel Bourne, where I discovered it.

The Heintzman was an upright grand. Meaning it had a full-sized soundboard, the same as a baby grand. Except that the soundboard was positioned vertically, making it stand taller than the usual console-type upright piano. It had a deep brown, walnut shell that showed signs of its age. The finish was dull and dark with a nick here, a scratch there. When you lifted the cover, the words "Heintzman, Toronto" were embossed in gold lettering. It stood out against the dark walnut background. Some of the keys looked like the teeth of a professional Canadian hockey player who never wore a helmet. None were missing, but there were some sharp edges. The dampening system creaked like the hinges on an old cabinet door when you pressed the pedals. There was a natural reverb to the squeaks as they bounced around inside the shell. The felt on the hammers of the piano had been compressed from the years of use, giving it a rather bright tone as they struck the strings.

In its early years, the piano probably had a much warmer sound. But it had a beautiful sonic spectrum due to its full-size soundboard. Especially the rich low end, as it resonated on the natural wood floors of the red room. I loved playing it. It had as much character as the old house it sat in. I would check in on the Heintzman on our visits as the years passed, in the summertime and on holidays. Gayle always appreciated hearing it being played. Occasionally, I would play a chord with a bit more color than the rest, and her eyebrows would go up. I'm sure it reminded her of the hours her son spent working out his giftings while she listened in the kitchen. Reid, an accomplished pianist, spent hours in front of it as he grew up. Apparently, from time to time, he would get lazy with his practicing. When he did, Gayle would pelt him with a wet dishrag from the adjacent kitchen. But by this time, both of her kids had married and relocated stateside. The old house was more often quiet than not, making our time together there much more valuable.

Chapter 12

Westdel Bourne was a large house. It took a good bit of sweat and determination to keep the place up, especially to Dutch standards. When my father-in-law announced his retirement in 2010, there was a sense that change was on the horizon. As much as Mr. Fun and Double G loved the serenity and beauty of Westdel Bourne, the cost of upkeep and the physical demand for maintenance became impractical. We began to savor every moment we had there, knowing that the clock was ticking. Ashley and I had made so many memories in that old house. It's where we met. It's where I proposed . . . and then there was the rehearsal dinner. There had been a lot of laughter and love that had transpired within those walls. God had done so much in us there.

Rick and Gayle divulged their plans to downsize and buy a small place in Chatham, where Gayle grew up. They would be closer to extended family there. The house would soon be placed on the market. The realization that it would eventually belong to someone else came with a sense of heaviness, even though we all acknowledged its sale as the right thing to do. Preparations for the move were set in motion.

Unbeknownst to us, Rick and Gayle had made a decision that would have a substantial impact on our home life. To our astonishment, Gayle confided in Ashley that they wanted to pass the Heintzman on to our family. We knew how much that piano meant to her. We couldn't believe it. The news came with a twinge of guilt, knowing how much time Ashley's brother, Reid, had spent playing it. Reid's family had inherited a piano from his wife's parents a few years before. It didn't make sense for them to have two. We were next in line. I was ecstatic.

The idea that an instrument like that, so full of unique character, so loaded with a sense of family legacy, would be readily accessible to our family made my heart race. In an unexpected way, it touched on the same place in me that the loss of the St. Charles house had wounded years before. A beautiful sense of grace washed over me when I thought about it. The shiny baby grand piano of my childhood that was lost in the pain of my parents' divorce was going to be replaced with the Heintzman, which had played such a wonderfully essential role the weekend we got married. I loved every blemish on the finish, all the squeaks and creeks that the years had borne. To me, the Heintzman was a symbol of longevity and faithfulness. Consistency. It's what I wanted for Ashley and me and the family that God would entrust us with. It was such a departure from the pain of what I had experienced in my own family.

It just so happened that the timing of my father-in-law's retirement coincided with our decision to move from Nashville to Phoenix to work at CCV. I can't prove it, but I believe that all Canadians are born with a deeply embedded instinct to migrate south in the winter months. It's not just the geese. I started to notice a spring in Mr. Fun's step and a glimmer in his eye as he considered the prospect of a guestroom in the desert during the winter months. It was as if he had served a long sentence in a cold Siberian prison and could see the light at the end of the tunnel. He started spending more time polishing his golf clubs, and his wardrobe began to take a subtle shift toward Tommy

Bahama. "Michael, you don't have to shovel sunshine," he said with a grin. My son-in-law stock skyrocketed.

All of Ashley's extended family packed into Westdel Bourne for the last Christmas that would be spent there. It was bittersweet. After Christmas dinner, Ashley's uncles and cousins helped us move the piano from its place under the skylight in the red room to the U-Haul trailer we rented for its transport. We all strained as we lifted it over the old threshold into the cold night air, doing our best to avoid adding any additional character to the finish. We carried the piano down the old cobblestone path that connected the gravel driveway to the house, avoiding falling in the snow. Gayle stood in the doorway and watched it leave the house. Her breath vaporized in the winter air just as it had when she had played it in the cold garage of the Chatham house as a little girl. She was acknowledging the end of a season and the welcoming of another.

By that time, Ashley and I had welcomed Brody into the world. I remember the nurse at the hospital instructing me on how to swaddle him tightly before putting him to sleep at night. I felt uncomfortable with how tight she wrapped him up, tucking his arms down away from his face so they wouldn't creep out. I remember tugging on the strap that tightened his tiny frame into the car seat and snapping it into the base in the back seat of our car when we brought him home from the hospital. Our family has never been the same since. He became a part of us, a fellow traveler on the adventure.

Brody was there with us at Westdel when the piano was loaded out. There's no comparing an inanimate object made of wood, brass, and ivory with the miracle of a human soul. Even the most ornately crafted instrument doesn't hold a candle to what God does when He knits a person together in the mysterious depths of the womb. Fingers and toes, skin and bone animated by His very breath, live in a category all their own. But in a similar way, we welcomed the Heintzman into our family that night. We wrapped it tightly in packing blankets and strapped it snugly into the trailer, distributing its weight evenly across the axles of the trailer. It joined our story that night just as Broderick Michael had not long before.

The Heintzman saw the end of our years in Nashville. It would end up in the front room of our Phoenix house, where it sat as we welcomed both Bentley and Beckett into our home for the first time. I played lullabies on it as we tried to get them to sleep, swaddled tightly as their older brother had been. It lived there through the deep sense of betrayal that I felt in my relationship with Ben. I remember seeing it when I walked in the door after being let go, wondering what I was going to say to Ashley. There were times in that season when I found myself sitting in front of its keys, playing and praying in desperation in the front room, just as my dad had done years before in the St. Charles house. It sat as a quiet spectator, listening in on the angst-filled conversations and prayers that would eventually lead our family to Eleven22 in Jacksonville. Before the piano joined our family, it hadn't traveled more than a hundred miles, but by the time the Heintzman landed in the front room of the Jacksonville house, it had seen the better part of the continental United States. I say house on purpose. It didn't feel like home. We hadn't yet lived life in it like we had in Phoenix or Nashville.

The Jacksonville house was built in the late '90s by the same family from which we purchased it. I had the privilege of meeting Miss Robin, who raised her family there. She happened to be in the house during one of our viewings. It was home to her, and she wasn't shy about letting me know it. By this time, all her kids had grown and moved out, and her husband and lifetime sweetheart, Jerry, had passed away. She had done her best as a widow to keep up with the maintenance, but it was proving to be too difficult. She made the decision to put it on the market to downsize, much like Mr. Fun and Double G had in London. Amidst her sadness in seeing it go, she graciously expressed that she was happy that we would have the opportunity to raise our family there. As she walked me through the house, she subtly hinted that she was an interior decorator. My surroundings confirmed that it was true.

The house was filled with all the frills you would expect from a passionate décor expert firmly entrenched in the 1990s. It was apparent that Miss Robin was a wallpaper connoisseur. Every possible pattern that you could imagine could be found on the walls, from the boldest floral to the most subtle pinstripe. There were layers upon layers of it, as we would eventually discover. One could argue that the actual square footage of the home had been skewed by the wallpaper's thickness on the walls. The wallpaper was accentuated by window treatments that looked like bridesmaid dresses from the 1980s. Large poofs of satin in deep sage and maroon were strewn about the place without a neutral color to be found. The bathrooms featured mint green marble countertops and shiny brass fixtures that looked as though they had been lifted from the palace of Versailles. As Miss Robin walked me from room to room, I hemmed and hawed at her artistic vision. In my mind, all I saw was dollar signs and sweat equity, but the house had good bones. It was open and naturally bright.

What eventually sold us on it was the view that hit you upon entrance. You were immediately confronted with a massive seven-panel curved window that looked out the back toward a Georgia pine-lined fairway. It sat on a water hazard that flanked the ninth hole of a public golf course. The giant window made the room feel like the bridge of a giant cruise ship. I knew immediately that I could think good thoughts in a room like that. There were sunrises to be taken in and morning conversations with God to be had. It was the new front room, the perfect place for the Heintzman.

We moved into the house on August 19, 2016, and started peeling wallpaper. It was an immense task. How do you eat an elephant? One bite at a time. This was an unusually large and sticky elephant. Westdel Bourne had taught us what home was supposed to feel like. We wanted so much to create that sense of stability in our new city. As we soaked and scraped the walls, we attempted to emotionally connect with our new surroundings. To this day, I still can't decide which process was more tedious: the soaking and scraping or trying to make the emotional connection.

Then, as God's providence would have it, on October 7th, the official Florida meteorological welcoming committee showed up at our front door in the form of Hurricane Matthew as it bellowed through Jacksonville. When it left, it took some of our newly purchased house with it. It was a historic storm, having been fifty years since the Jacksonville coast had experienced anything of its magnitude. The beautiful view out the back window was littered with torn shingles and debris. Gale-force winds cleared a twenty-foot by twenty-foot section of the roof peak over the living room down to the plywood, and rainwater was leaking down the interior walls. From the inside, it looked like the house itself was weeping. Giant tears were streaming down its drywall cheeks. As the storm crept eastward over the Atlantic, I crawled up on the roof with a giant blue tarp, doing my best to mitigate the remaining tailwinds. I felt like Forrest Gump's legless Lieutenant Dan strapped up to the crow's nest of the shrimp boat, shaking his fist at God, saying, "Is this all You've got?!" I risked my life affixing the giant blue tarp to the bare patch to avoid any further interior water damage. I pinned it down with a few forty-pound bags of topsoil, which was all I had on hand. The wind eventually overpowered the gravity that held the bags down to what was left of the roof, causing them to drop like atomic bombs on the back porch. Each bag exploded with a loud *bang* as it hit the ground, adding to the mess. It was a warzone.

When the storm had passed, Ashley and I did our best to deal with the damage. We found ourselves being pulled into the seedy underbelly of the insurance industry. On behalf of the company that held our homeowner's policy, an adjuster, who looked like a card-carrying member of the

Cosa Nostra, showed up to assess the damage. After five minutes on our roof, he promptly produced a handwritten estimate that sat $300 under our deductible. He grinned as he passed me the paperwork. Whatever fix was required would seemingly be on our dime.

Around the same time, we received a knock on the front door from the chairman of the neighborhood HOA. He was an older gentleman who had joined the ranks of the neighborhood political establishment in his retirement years. He was known for scouring the neighborhood for potential violations while walking his miniature Scottie dog. After pushing through the formality of inquiring about our general well-being post-hurricane, he got straight to the point. He made sure we were aware that a partial repair of our roof would be out of the question on account of the disparity in the color match between the new and existing shingles. It was something the golfers on the public course just couldn't stand for. We were between a rock and a hard place. The rock was the crooked adjuster, and the hard place was the hard-nosed president of the HOA. To appease all parties, the Olsons (fresh off a move from the desert where hurricanes were a rarity) found ourselves on the hook for fronting the cost for the replacement of our entire roof out of pocket. The bill would be in the tens of thousands of dollars.

Ashley and I couldn't believe it. In a move of desperation, I called every local roofer I could find, searching for an alternative. Miraculously, I was introduced to the world of the *public adjuster*, a term of which I was not yet familiar. Apparently, in the state of Florida, laws had been passed to ensure the possibility of neutral advocacy for people in situations like ours. After a few more calls, we had found our inside man. In no time, John Longfellow, our newly acquired public adjuster, took the Cosa Nostra insurance industry to task. In minutes, John had forced the insurance company's hand to agree to an estimate that was well over our deductible. John had given us a line of sight on a completely new roof for the cost of our deductible, meeting the HOA's demands. The news came like a ray of sunlight beaming down through the dark clouds that hovered over our home, clad with the giant blue tarp.

CHAPTER 13

Ashley and I did our best to create a sense of home in Jacksonville. We hung family pictures on the walls that weren't affected by the hurricane. We planted flowers in the yard. We enrolled Brody in second grade at the elementary school across the street. With each successive step, we moved toward making the Jacksonville house feel like Westdel Bourne, safe and stable. This was certainly for our own sake, but now the stakes were much higher. We knew that we had three young, moldable souls under our care. Broderick Michael, Bentley Reid, and Beckett James needed a place to grow up that would provide them with a sure footing in the process of maturing into the men they were meant to be. This is something to which I was particularly sensitive and attentive, for good reason.

My mom and dad's divorce was finalized shortly after he left Elmhurst for California to pursue the escape-hatch life he had been building in his mind during my teenage years. It's unsettling to think about how long he let that scenario percolate inside of him. By the time the paperwork was signed, Ashley and I had already been married for five years. Not long after it was official, my dad remarried. I found out about it from my sister after the fact. Apparently, the ceremony took place in a small venue in Las Vegas. A far cry from the A-frame of my boyhood. He and his new wife, Linda, moved into a townhouse in Orange County, California. He and Linda came to visit us within the first year of their wedding. They slept in the guest room of our Nashville house. She was a divorcee of a wealthy Los Angeles real estate developer. Who knows what kind of pain she brought into their relationship? Only God. During the visit, I found myself trying to build an exact timeline of when they met. The details were hazy at best, and even if I could, I'm not sure I wanted to. They both giggled, huddling together on our couch as my dad told stories about his new relationship with Linda's grandkids. I smiled in response and squeezed Ashley's hand. There was nothing about it that felt right. It was a foreign land, and I didn't know the language.

Linda and my dad were married for less than two years when the bottom fell out. The alternate reality that my dad had so delicately constructed over the years, the one that he had pinned his hopes on to fulfill his unmet desires and cover his pain, was a mirage. He chased it all the way to the Pacific, where it disappeared into thin air. Instead of living out his fantasies of intimacy and connection with a new lover, a new family, and a new city, he was left in a pit of deeper isolation than he had previously been in. All the "new" that he had idolized had turned into a solitary confinement cell. The letdown shattered his psyche. I never heard from Linda again.

My mom was still living in our family home when she received a phone call informing her that Dad had been admitted to a mental institution in LA. She passed the information on to my brother, my sister, and me. She let us know that she was going to make the long drive from Chicago's west side to pick him up and bring him home. I can't imagine the thoughts and emotions she would navigate as she sat in the car by herself, driving west. Hours and miles filtering through grief, loss, and the potential of a new start. Thirty years and three children with a man whom she had loved, who she had hurt, and who had hurt her. It all rattled around in her brain. Surely this was close to what rock bottom felt like, if not rock bottom itself. The desire for redemption, for intimacy reconciled, had to be there.

It would be dishonest for me to say that a flicker of hope didn't rise up in my gut as I pictured them side by side in the car, heading back home. So much time had gone by, and so much wreckage had piled up. Even in its high improbability, my deep longing for the innocence of my boyhood groaned for them to rediscover peace. I wanted it for them and for me. I wanted the conversations around the family table to come back. I wanted what we had before the darkness crept in. I knew it was close to impossible, but my spirit kept asking God for it, groaning as the days went by. But I was too afraid to say anything out loud.

Dad stayed at home for a month or so while Mom took care of him. It had become apparent that to cope with it all, he had developed an unhealthy dependency on prescription medication: anxiety meds and antidepressants. The extremity of it landed him in the emergency room of Elmhurst Memorial Hospital in medical and psychiatric duress. He would later describe the event to me in vivid detail and in a rage of emotion. The darkness that had taken root in him had such a hold; he couldn't break free from it alone. It was decided that he should spend some time in a faith-based detox clinic in southern Florida. Perhaps if he could get his body and his mind freed up from the effects of the overuse of the medication, he could find the footing to move forward.

He went through the program and came back to Elmhurst, but he and my mom never found common ground. The glimmer of hope that kindled in my heart at their improbable reuniting turned out to be just as much a mirage as the alternate reality he had concocted for himself. He moved into a small apartment across town. One of his former clients, a well-respected custom home builder in the city, gave him a job as a staff architect. He knew that my dad needed help. He was right. My dad poured himself into his work. Men do that. He tried to find a sense of belonging in a few local churches, but the prospect of living authentically in community with others was too costly. He was unknown.

It's uncomfortable to think of him getting in his car by himself on a Sunday morning, pulling into the parking lot of a new church, and trying to find a place to sit. Such a drastic shift from what was. He had already experienced integration between faith and relationship at the deepest level. He had made such an investment of soul and sweat in the faith community at Northwest. Those days were so full of life and color and music . . . and fire. The organ bench on the side of the platform seemed to be a million miles away. Now he was a spectator with a broken heart.

From time to time, we would connect on the phone. At first, the conversations were always awkward and sparse. I am ashamed to say that they would often escalate into an angry tirade. Two bruised and battered souls grinding against each other. Like father, like son. The sparks flew. We both expected the other to give something that neither of us could. We were too broken. Pharisees with planks in our eyes, blinded to the true state of each other. This went on for years. As time passed, I noticed his spirit weakened. There was less anger in our conversations. It was some combination of the mysterious work of the Spirit and the effect of sheer fatigue from the heavy burden he was carrying. I'm still not sure which was which. To me, it seemed more like the latter, but I can't be certain. I was longing for the anger to be replaced by what I needed from my father: steady fortitude, biblical meekness, and restrained strength. Instead, his voice began to weaken when we connected on the phone. It was airy, and it drifted higher in pitch. His words became soft and affectionate. I didn't know how to process it. I was simultaneously fed by his affirmation and alienated by his passivity. Ironically, there were times when I missed the sharpness of his tongue before he started to fade. I craved a masculine edge, the same one I strove to provide for my sons. I was conflicted. I needed a dad, and he was the only one I had.

Dad's last visit with Ashley and me was in Phoenix in the spring of 2015. We had just had our third son, Beckett, and Dad wanted to meet him. I picked him up from the airport and took him to our home in the northwest corner of the city. As my dad's 6'4" frame entered the front door, Ashley stood in front of him holding his tiny grandson. Beckett's older brothers, Brody and Bentley, were there flanking Mom on the left and right. Brody was six and Bentley was two. There was a glimmer of light in his eyes as he took us in. His physical stature hadn't changed; he was still a giant man. But he was too weak to channel the depth of soul that he had accessed in earlier days. He had given so much, lived so hard. Things had gone so far awry. But he caught a glimpse of something as he looked at Ashley and me, and our three boys. It was something he had tried to run from, but ironically, in that moment, I could tell it was deeply fulfilling. He was dad and grandpa. It crept down into his deep places. I could see him drink it in like a cup of cold water quenching a desperate thirst. Even amidst all the fallout of what had transpired, he had a primal desire to know that his life had a sense of lasting significance.

I had a visceral reaction as he reached out to hold Beckett. I didn't realize all that was happening at the time, but looking back, I now have more clarity. There we were: three generations of Olsons altogether, each born with a deep, God-shaped hole, yet at different stages of trying to figure out how to move ahead. Our three boys, whose youthful innocence and naivety were epitomized by young

Beckett. He was diapered and helpless, yet with a blue-sky future. My dad, weathered and weak, was trying to make sense of what was behind him. I was caught in the middle. Young enough to hold on to optimism, but old enough to have experienced pain. I had a deep urge to protect Beckett from my dad as he cradled him in his arms. I wanted to snatch him away while thinking, *Son, hold on to that sense of innocence and simplicity for as long as you can. Don't ever give it up. I can't protect you from what is ahead, but I want to.* I didn't say it out loud, but it echoed in my heart.

My dad slept for most of that visit. When he wasn't sleeping, he was lost in technology. He seemed enslaved to YouTube. Watching it was the path of least resistance. There were only two things that pulled him out of the daze that he was in. The first was his work. He was designing a building that would become a car dealership for the company where he worked. When he talked about it, I could see shadows of the pride that he had in his work designing those grand mansions in years past. It was a welcome sight. The second was the old upright piano in our front room, the Heintzman. On a few occasions, my dad would saunter into the formal living room where it sat. A rush of familiarity hit me as he trusted his weight to the bench and his hands crept over the keys. It's fascinating how sound and smell trigger memory. They are a time machine transporting you back to memories that exist in the far recesses of your mind. As the chords my dad played poured into my ears, I was transported back to the front room of the house on St. Charles. The music came out slower, and his fingers fumbled from time to time, but I could tell he still had it. The music was still in him.

It was clear that addiction to prescription medication still had a hold on him. His eyes were cloudy, and his thoughts were slow. I still remember him sprawled out on the couch in our living room, snoring with his tablet bobbing up and down on his chest. It made me sad as much as it made me angry. I would pull Ashley aside and rant, "Can you believe this? He hasn't seen his grandkids for years, and all he does is sleep while he's here?" She knew my anger didn't help. She brought us both to recognize the sadness in it. It was a more appropriate reaction. He was sick and we knew it. He was caught in a trap, and he was doing the best he could. But even with all of that, something magical happened when he played the Heintzman. It was weighty. It was spiritual, and I was glad for it.

We worked our way through the rest of the visit. I kept my emotions in check in our conversations. I knew the slightest misplaced word could set off a devastating chain of events that would only exasperate the situation, leaving us both with a deep sense of regret. I kept things on the surface level to avoid additional pain. I'm not sure he had the vitality to sustain any further fallout. When I dropped him off at the airport for the flight back home, we both said, "I love you." We briefly embraced before he turned to head toward his gate. I had a sense that his time was limited. I didn't know what to do. I played out different scenarios in my mind. A family intervention, more time in a detox clinic, or deep psychiatric care. I couldn't see a path toward him responding to any of them, and every scenario seemed to lead to more relational strife that would eventually push us farther apart. My inaction led me into deep guilt. It was paralyzing.

My brother, David, brought his family to Chicago during the fall of 2016 to celebrate Thanksgiving with my dad and some of our extended family who still lived in the area. He also had a sense of what was happening with my dad. I think it prompted him to take the trip. He was living in Kansas City at the time, so the drive was doable. By that time, our family home on St. Charles Road was sold in the divorce. All the stuff from my childhood went along with it, most notably the instruments in the front room. My dad still had the organ. He crammed it in the living room of his small apartment across town. The Yamaha baby grand piano I had grown up with was being offered on consignment in a local piano shop. When we found out about it, something died inside my siblings and me.

My mom had relocated to the Orlando area, and my sister was in Minneapolis. We were all over the country without the sense of tether that we had before the house sold. We reached out to each other on the phone on Thanksgiving Day, wishing each other well. My brother and my dad had ended up at my Aunt Marilyn's house across the Wisconsin border for the holiday. Marilyn was his twin sister, whose husband had retired from teaching in the public schools on the north side of Chicago. Among the things I was grateful for that day was the time my brother spent with my dad, and the fact that my dad decided to spend the day with his family up in Wisconsin. I hated imagining him alone. When I heard the commotion at Aunt

Marilyn's house through my brother's phone, I felt a sense of ease. I knew things hadn't gotten less complicated. In fact, I knew that my brother was working through all the complexities of spending time with my dad himself. David has always had a tender heart and a spirit of empathy. I knew my dad was benefiting from his company.

My brother and his family had planned to leave the Chicago area on Saturday morning after the holiday to make it home for his weekend work obligations. He had decided to make one more trip to visit my dad that morning, before they left, to see if there were any last-minute things he could help him with. He left his family at the hotel where they were staying and drove to his apartment. He used the key my dad had given him to open the front door. It was quiet when he walked in. My brother walked down the short hallway and pushed the door open to my dad's bedroom. He found him dead on the floor.

I wasn't there to experience it. My brother bore the initial blow, and he bears the mental scar as a result. We've since talked about it, the un-erasable image of seeing your father lying lifeless by himself on the carpet. The odd, stale odor in the air. The fading color in his face and hands. To this day, it creeps up in deep conversations between us, sometimes with great untamable and undefinable emotion. We don't talk much. We talk about this even less. But in many ways, it has become definitive to both of us. In all honesty, the knowledge of the pain of my dad's last years and the fact that he died the way he did has pushed my brother away from God. At least the God we were raised in the fear of by our father under the

A-frame. I've wrestled too. I've grappled with that same God over it. I'm doing it right now as I type. I'm sitting in a crowded coffee shop across from the Atlantic Ocean in Jacksonville with my AirPods in, trying to decide if I need to grab my sunglasses to hide what's about to pour out of my eyes. He died over six years ago, and recounting the details still churns up the depths in me. As this story continues, I'll share where that journey has led me. But for now, the fact is that my dad, the mansion designer, the organ bench temple builder of my boyhood, who once carried the capacity to channel a most uncommon depth of soul to create beauty, took his last earthly breath alone on the floor of a one-bedroom apartment.

My brother, reeling from the reality of it, began to take the appropriate steps with an odd surge of adrenaline. I still don't know how he did what he did. He jumped into the role of the oldest brother like a soldier under fire, dodging bullets and taking ground. He made the phone calls and alerted the authorities. The news began to spread. I heard about it from my mom. Her voice broke on the phone as she spoke. She referred to him as *daddy*. As she said the word, I experienced a severe jolt. Whiplash. A sudden presentness with the way I heard that word in the security of our home as a little boy, before the darkness set in, colliding with the coldness of the here and now. I had no category for it.

After dealing with the immediate fallout, my brother drove his family back to Kansas City. He promptly turned around and headed back to Chicago to do what needed to be done. Part of that was attending to what would happen with my dad's body and the autopsy. He worked with the local authorities to ensure that everything was taken care of. The Cook County Coroner concluded that the cause of death was "accidental overdose of prescription medication." There was no surprise in it, but that didn't lighten the impact.

My dad's death and the cause of it hung over the following days like a thick fog. Our family was scattered around the country. We hadn't been together for a long time, both in the physical and emotional sense. Even if we could grieve together as a family, none of us would know how. It was so multi-dimensional. There was still the grief of a lost sense of mom and dad and of the dissolved marriage. It was a grief of losing a sense of home and security. There was the sorrow over what seemed to be the endless spiral of my dad's later years. The constancy of the bottom dropping out. Just when you thought it had reached its lowest, a sucker punch caught you by surprise. And now, the new finality of the grief that he was gone. It was like the smoldering of the A-frame that Jimmy and I had sat in front of years before. The raging fire of my dad's years of demon fighting had been laid to rest. It was as if we were on the swings across the parking lot, trying to take it in, watching the burnt hymnal pages drift in the breeze. We were completely lost. We didn't have a place to grieve. There was no physical address in Chicago other than the vacant one-bedroom apartment that my dad was renting. That was the farthest thing from home that any of us could possibly imagine.

Helen, died years later. We were living in Nashville at the time, and I was playing music on the road for a living. I made the decision to miss the funeral. I'm ashamed to say it. I regret it. My mom's parents were never in the picture. I didn't know their names. I couldn't even describe what they looked like. We weren't a close family. There was no well of family experience to draw from. The first funeral I would attend would be the loss of the most influential man in my life.

It felt like I had run headfirst into an impassible barricade, and I was dizzy from impact. I could wrap my head around the idea of pain, especially when it came because of poor decision-making. I even had some sense of how God could use pain. I had seen people transformed by it. To a measure, I had experienced it myself. Death seemed different than pain. I tried to dig underneath it and pick it up, to bear it on my shoulders. It was too heavy; I didn't have the strength. It was too far-reaching for my mind to process and too toxic for my soul to touch on its own. I began to understand that if I relegated myself to the natural, to the material, I would drown in a sea as ominous and expansive as the night sky out the airplane window. It felt like weeping and gnashing of teeth. I was standing on the edge of something or somewhere. A place that, up to this point, I hadn't yet encountered. I knew I had to move forward through it. I couldn't stay where I was. But it was in territory I didn't have permission or power to traverse alone.

I began to realize that I had spent the entirety of my life in proximity to the resurrection. Dangerously close. I had confessed and been baptized. I had even written songs about it . . . about Him, Jesus the Nazarene. Yet I had never needed Him the way I needed Him right then. I had never felt the chasm between the living and the dead so intimately. In a way I had never considered, I could tell that Jesus was in between, mediating, advocating, and speaking a better word than the blood of Abel. His person began to take a fuller sense of dimension and significance. He was the Morningstar piercing the overwhelming darkness. There at 30,000 feet, I began to juxtapose the shortcomings of my father; all the pain and dysfunction, all the addiction and anger, all the false hopes that the worst was over, only to discover a lower low with the power of *Tetelestai*—it is finished. I was overtaken by the reality that at that moment my dad was standing whole in the presence of a Holy God with nothing to offer but the finished work of Christ. Whatever merit he could have brought to the table with his years of service had been spent. His inheritance was squandered. He was too weak to present an argument on his own behalf. He was poor in spirit, but that was enough. Jesus, his older brother, had taken the helm and carried him into paradise like the thief propped up like a scarecrow who recognized who He was in the eleventh hour. He bridged the disparity between God's holiness and my dad's brokenness with love to spare. This was not limp religious sentiment. Nor was it cold, stoic doctrine. It was Christ in us, the hope of glory.

The next day, my heart sped up as my brother and I walked through the doors of Northwest. The building was showing signs of age. It was rundown and dirty. Everything seemed smaller as I took it in, about half the size I remembered it being. Several updates were made in an attempt to keep up with the times. The lobby had been expanded to include a small coffee shop with high-top round tables. The platform of the sanctuary had been gutted out and rebuilt to facilitate a more modern worship experience. The fake stained glass that had been installed as a nod to the original A-frame had been covered up by a stage set. The choir loft was gone, and there was no organ on the right side of the platform.

Membership had dwindled in numbers as time had passed. I'm sure it left the pastoral leadership in a state of crisis on how to care for the property. There was a general heaviness about the place. The air was stale, unlike the way I remembered it from my childhood. I could sense that the years that had come and gone were as complicated for Northwest as they had been for the Olsons. But I recognized the places where God had stirred my heart as a young boy, like the dark stairwell in the basement where I hid while I wept in God's presence.

The service was to be held in the large youth room upstairs. This was a part of the original structure that had weathered the fire. My dad had re-purposed the space by consolidating classrooms for the growing youth ministry. During our high school years, my sister and I attended youth services in the same room. It was a more appropriate size for the number of people in attendance than the large room downstairs. Upon entering the room, I made eye contact with my mom. She was there with my sister. She promptly walked over and embraced my brother and me. My sister and I exchanged an embrace as well. My mom has never been short on words a day in her life, but at that moment, she was reserved with them. What words were shared were sparse and hushed. The four of us stood there together in the quiet. We hadn't been together in the same physical space for quite a while. Life had pulled us in different directions.

My mom was (and is) averse to any kind of change. If she had her way, we would all still be living in the St. Charles house, as if nothing had happened. But the divorce forced her to change. The house was gone, and now Dad was too. I can't speak for my brother and sister, but I was looking for change. Looking back, I can see that when I left home for college, I was running away from something. I never really went back. Home was a place of hurt. Being there, in that circle with my family, made me realize that there are some things that you can't really run away from. They have a way of catching up with you. There is a fine line between avoiding pain and living through it without letting it define you. The latter is way more difficult. Yet for all of this, we found ourselves sharing this moment in the church where we were raised, breathing each other's air.

My mom started to open up as familiar faces began to trickle in. Even through the divorce, she had maintained a sense of connection with my dad's family. They worked through the pain of my dad's latter years together. In many ways, it was the only extended family she ever had. There was Aunt Marilyn and Uncle Dan, along with their three grown children. My dad's older brothers were all there with their spouses and children, most of whom I was largely unfamiliar with. My mom graciously greeted each one with an embrace.

As the hour of the service grew closer, a remarkable thing began to happen. The room started to fill up with the familiar faces of my childhood faith family. People I had seen my mom and dad worship alongside began to materialize out of thin air. These were the colorful characters that I would spy on behind the coat racks in the lobby of the old A-frame. Everyone had aged, but they were all still the same. As they filtered in, I saw my mom's countenance begin to change. Even amidst the heaviness of the occasion, there was a sublime sense of joy in the reconnections. If grief was to be had, it was better shared in a community like this. The reality was that none of us (my mom, brother, sister, and I) had seen or communicated with many of these folks for years. But there was a beautiful feeling of familiarity as we gathered in that place. Each one had a collection of memories behind their eyes. Times reveling in God's presence in God's house, together. Times of music and dancing, of loud prayer in foreign tongues and deafening silence in the heaviness of God's glory. The soundtrack to a vast percentage of those memories was created by my dad sitting at the organ to the right. We were all stirred by it, by the soul that poured through his hands and feet.

Everyone found their seats as the service began, with my family in the front row. We prayed. We read the Psalms, and we remembered. We acknowledged my dad's beautifully complicated journey as we sat in the place of worship that was born out of his great mind. Some of this was material; the physicality of common spaces designed for prayer and fellowship, and the gathering of the saints. A greater portion was spiritual, manifested in the atmosphere he created through his gift of song. We sang together. We welcomed harmony. It had a way of soothing the sting of loss. My brother, my sister, and I joined together singing hymns and spiritual songs that had meant a lot to my dad and, in turn, to the community of faith. My mom beamed from the row. Her rich alto voice joined in, now with a widened vibrato. It rediscovered its place in God's house. I walked up to the podium and opened my Bible to the Gospel of John.

> *Now a certain man was ill, Lazarus of Bethany, in the village of Mary and her sister Martha . . . Now Jesus loved Martha and her sister and Lazarus . . . Martha said to Jesus, "Lord, if you had been here, my brother would not have died. But even now I know that whatever you ask from God, God will give you." Jesus said to her, "Your brother will rise again." Martha said to him, "I know that he will rise again in the resurrection on the last day." Jesus said to her, "I am the resurrection and the life. Whoever believes in me, though he die, yet shall he live, and everyone who lives and believes in me shall never die. Do you believe this?"* (John 11:1-26)

As I unpacked the story, I remembered the brightness of the stars piercing the darkness of the night sky as I looked out the plane window the day before.

CHAPTER 14

When I landed in Jacksonville after the funeral, I was as emotionally depleted as I had ever been. I dragged myself from the arrival gate to the economy parking lot, wheeling my bag in tow, and threw my weight into the driver's seat of the car. My physical man was straining under the intensity of all that had transpired. My heart was beating slow and heavy. My arms felt like they each weighed 200 pounds as I reached up for the steering wheel. The Phoenix loss, complete immersion in unfamiliar faces and places in Jacksonville, the storm, and now my dad's death.

As I pulled into our neighborhood and made the slight left curve toward our house at the end of the street, the blue tarp on the roof came into view. I parked in the driveway and sank even deeper into my seat, slouching my shoulders forward as I lay my head on the steering wheel and sat in the quiet. After a few deep breaths, I got out of the car and sauntered to the front door. I pushed it open and took a brief survey around the house. The kitchen walls were in various stages of deconstruction from all the wallpaper removal. It looked like an onion in the process of being peeled. The paint on the walls of the living room was starting to bubble from the water that leaked in after the hurricane. The dank smell of moisture hung in the air, and Miss Robin's remaining Florida décor seemed more gaudy than usual.

Ashley appeared around the corner and rushed to welcome me. Her soft lips landed on mine as she held me for a second, acknowledging the gravity of what must have happened in Chicago. The quiet didn't last long. "Daddy's home!" rang out from the other end of the house. The two oldest appeared out of nowhere and jumped on my back, wrapping their arms around my neck. I knelt and squeezed them tight. I carried them in to greet their younger brother, who was less mobile. He looked up at me and smiled. This was home. Not the house with the disheveled walls and blue tarp on the roof. But these souls that God had knit together, this family. I remembered the feeling I got when I saw Ashley for the first time in London and how quickly I knew we would share our lives. I remember welcoming each of our sons into the world on the day they were born. If I had any people in the world to call my own, any consistent community and fellowship at all, it was these standing in front of me. I stood there in the wake of seeing my dad's body lying motionless in his coffin and looked at Ashley, Brody, Bentley, and Beckett. There was so much warmth in them, so much vitality. They stood out amidst the wreckage like a blazing lighthouse on a dark and rocky shore.

Simultaneously, a surge of immense gratitude and grave responsibility washed over me. I was Ashley's husband, the only one she'd ever have. When asked if she would commit herself to me in the face of anything that life could throw at us, she agreed. I did the same. Now we were living in the depths of the commitment we had made. And then there were the three boys who shared our blood. Each one is uniquely and purposefully crafted. They are the most beautiful creatures I have ever seen. There was so much possibility before them. In time, their tiny shoulders would broaden, their young minds would evolve, and their souls would develop the same depth that their grandpa had. The depth he passed on to me. I knew they needed a guide; someone they could trust. Someone who could help them harness their passions correctly, to leverage them in the right way and for the right purposes. I was more aware at that moment than I had ever been of how valuable a father was, and I was the only one they would ever know.

Ashley and I took the boys upstairs and tucked them into their beds. I laid my hands on each one individually and prayed a prayer of blessing, speaking each of their names aloud to God. There was no emotion to muster. There was no rise and fall in the tone of my voice, no added drama to try to convince God that I needed Him. I believed that He already knew it. The prayers were far from the exuberant shouts of acclamation that I had heard echoing in the A-frame as a boy. Life had taken me to a place where I could no longer measure my level of connectedness to

Chapter 13

As we put one foot in front of the other, my brother leading the charge, a way forward started to emerge from the fog. It took a bit of digging, but we found a treasure, covered in a deep pile of irony. Although none of us, including my dad, had darkened its door for the better part of a decade, the only place that had any semblance of home for any of us (including my dad) was located on the corner of Wolf and Kensington in Mt. Prospect. We had all experienced an immense amount of pain and loss since the days that we called that place home, but home it still was. It was where my dad's instrument shorted out. Where the old A-frame that he inadvertently burnt to the ground used to stand, and where the new building that he designed now stood in its place. This is where my dad swayed and prayed. And this is where I met God. And so, it was mutually agreed upon that we would hold my dad's funeral at Northwest Assembly of God in Mt. Prospect, Illinois.

I got on an afternoon flight from Jacksonville to O'Hare by myself the day before the service. At the window seat, the sun began to set as the engines roared and the plane reached altitude. It was a clear night. On the horizon, an orange glow faded downward, giving way to a deep expanse of dark blue. The altitude made the stars pop against the darkening sky with unusual vividness. As I stared out the window, I did my best to quiet myself. To try to prepare for what I was walking into. I didn't have a lot of experience with death. My dad's father passed away from a heart attack when I was five years old. At the time, I was too young to understand what had happened. To this day, my memories of him are very limited. My dad's mother, Grandma

God by the way I felt. That building had burned down. I needed something deeper to rely on, something that didn't change. I spoke softly and steadily over their young spirits in the stillness of faith. When I was finished, Ashley and I went downstairs and fell asleep.

By the time my eyes opened the next morning, my mind had already picked up the worries I had laid down the previous night. I lay in bed, my mind racing as I processed all that had occurred. My fingers were fidgeting, and my pulse was quick. I got out of bed and walked around the house with a tightness in my chest. From time to time, a spell of dizziness would drift over me, forcing me to lose equilibrium. It seemed counterintuitive, but I felt as if I was coming down from a long adrenaline rush that had carried me through the previous season. We were months from the crisis in the desert, our cross-country move was in the rear-view mirror along with our close friends, and my dad had been interred in the memorial gardens alongside his father, where he had been buried decades before. My flesh felt a lull, and I capitalized on it. The crash created a ripple effect, resulting in enormous waves of anxiety. *Anxiety*. What a fascinating phenomenon.

The original Greek word in the New Testament, *merimnao*, which is used to convey anxiety, is a compound of two other Greek words: *merizo*, "to divide," and *nous*, "the mind." Anxiety is a departure from integration. Disunity within. In his attempt to define reality, seventeenth-century French Philosopher René Descartes tried to sum it all up with his famous phrase "cogito, ergo sum" (I think, therefore I am). The movement of modern rationalism followed, putting human reasoning in the pull position of defining reality. "Knowledge is king," he said. But, are we really that smart? What if the mind becomes divided? Or, what if there is a realm of reality that is beyond our capacity to understand?

Plato, in *The Allegory of the Cave*, put words on the idea that there is more to life than the immediate. He used mental pictures of fire and shadow to try to convey a hunch he had that there is something else out there beyond us. Something that can't be seen with the eye. A story behind the story that drives the immediate forward and gives it significance. Apparently, the ancient Greeks weren't that different from us. They felt the forces that function as the metanarrative to the literal and physical, and strove to understand them just like we do. Plato's philosophy isn't unique to his experience. Be it Jordan Peterson's quest for meaning, or John Mayer's muse revealing a quest for real love, it's all the same.

How about Bible folks? I have a hunch that for a minute, Adam (aka "dirt" animated by Spirit, formed in the image of God) didn't live in Plato's dichotomy between fire and shadow. He was created in a beautiful sense of harmonic unity between the two. Undivided, integrated with God and with himself. I don't think he struggled with anxiety for that brief, wonderful season. It didn't last long, just over two Genesis chapters to be exact. His physical and spiritual being were one and the same until the great schism of Genesis 3. The breach of trust between God and man built a Berlin wall of separation in all beings, save God alone. Since then, a lot of anxiety has followed.

What about Abraham? He was living a successful life in the material world. He was "very rich in livestock, in silver, and in gold" (Genesis 13:2). Yet he wrestled with an odd sense that something was going on beyond what his eyes could see, beyond what he could possess. He heard a voice altogether immaterial, making him promises that drew parallels between things he could see and things he couldn't. Stars and babies. He lived in the tug between the material and the immaterial for the rest of his life. Theologians call it faith, and it was credited to him as righteousness (Gen 15:6). I'm sure there were moments during the journey when he struggled with feeling divided, and it made him anxious.

Moses spent years in the anxious wilderness of the mundane before the paranormal burning bush confronted him. A historical event that is stunningly similar to Plato's idea. He didn't have the ability to comprehend it. It was on fire, but it wasn't being consumed. He was tending Jethro's sheep, taking care of what was present and at hand. All at once, the Horeb wilderness that he had grown so accustomed to was transformed into a portal leading to a completely different world. He found himself in conversation with Yahweh, the Holy. There was a season of time when he was the only one on earth with the knowledge that ultimate reality, God, had a name. He stuck his finger in the light socket of God's presence, and it jump-started his existence. It called him to integration. It even made him curious enough to ask to see the face behind the name. God knew he wasn't ready. (Images come to mind of Jack Nicholson screaming, "You can't handle the truth!" in a

Navy courtroom.) Not only that, but Yahweh had stuff for him to do. Stuff that would shatter the boundaries of the material. It freaked him out. Made him anxious enough to need a copilot, his brother Aaron.

Here's a question: If we are truly the byproduct of happenstance and primordial ooze, then why all the anxiety? Why the sense of quest? If the ultimate point of existence is defined purely by the ability to meet the incessant craving of the physical being for the sake of survival, be it appetite for food, sheltered sleep, or even sex (according to Freud), why are we dominated by a spirit of fear? Especially in the modern West, where this kind of anxiety seems to be the most prevalent. Over here, we are indulgent in our quest to meet the demand of our own appetites. We define ourselves by our appetites, and yet we are plagued.

Another question: Why is it that when we sit down for a meal with close family and friends, we are nourished on a deeper level than our physical bodies can afford when we get up from the table? Why does laughter in the common union of an intimate relationship feed us as much as meat and potatoes? Some could argue that laughter feeds us more, and at a deeper level. Why do we punish our most flagrant offenders by making them spend time by themselves? Solitary confinement. Or why would something as immaterially insignificant as a sharp word from a person of influence have the ability to wound so deeply? There must be more than meets the eye, a deeper level of existence.

As I was beaten down by the waves of anxiety that morning, I had no immediate physical needs that were unmet. I knew what I was going to eat and where I would sleep. There might have been a blue tarp on the roof, and the interior walls were lacking the sense of order preferred by my Dutch father-in-law, but we weren't in danger. I even had a brilliant ministry opportunity at Eleven22 that just happened to come with a bi-weekly paycheck and benefits. Apparently, I am more than my biology teacher led me to believe: a random collection of complex physical systems that were formed in some grand accident. I am soul and spirit wrapped in flesh, fearfully and wonderfully made. I was in an existential crisis that was blurring the lines between my physicality and my spirituality. The woundedness of one was spilling out into the reality of the other, wreaking havoc on the way I viewed the world.

In his beautiful memoir, *The Seven Story Mountain*, Catholic mystic Thomas Merton provides a haunting description of being overcome by the spirit of fear while on a New York City train car. It debilitated him physically to the point where he couldn't move. He described himself holding on to the bed frame of a high-rise Manhattan hotel room while he battled the sensation of being pulled out of the hotel room window by some unseen force. When I first read the story, I broke out in a cold sweat because it hit so close to home for me. That experience was a domino that tipped in his life. It eventually led him to a Cistercian monastery in rural Kentucky, where he would spend the rest of his life contemplating the union of all things in Jesus. I'm sure it was more peaceful and integrated than the subway car in downtown Manhattan.

And what is to be said about this Jesus? This Jesus who comes to us with a serene spirit of *shalom* in the midst of the anxiety-ridden valley between light and shadow, proclaiming the nearness of the kingdom of heaven. This Jesus, who demonstrates command over the immediate and mundane in water turned to wine, the multiplication of bread "ex nihilo", and the calming of the treacherous Galilee with the power of His word, while simultaneously wreaking of the same dirt as Adam, His predecessor. He healed lepers and turned them into men who were fully alive.

What do we make of His claim to be the light and bread, resurrection and life? What of His stunning command of the entirety of His personhood in forty days of wilderness fasting and "not my will but yours be done" (Luke 22:42) in the garden? Could it be that Plato's dichotomy of fire and shadow, Abraham's quest for the unseen, Moses's desire to see the glory, Jordan Peterson's thirst for meaning, and John Mayer's hunger for love are finally brought together in *Him*?

What if He is the culmination and unity of all being, as the writer of Colossians and Hebrews declares him to be? Upholding the universe by the word of his power . . . before all things and in him all things are held together. Is He the grand intersection that brings us back to the undivided being? Integration and convergence? The antithesis of anxiety. And if so, how would He accomplish such a thing? And what bearing does that have on me in the middle of my anxiety?

In the same pastoral letter that sent shockwaves through my soul in Glacier National Park, breaking the curse of deadly unforgiveness that killed my father, the apostle John gives the admonishment to flee the temptation to define our existence by the lust of the flesh, the lust of the eyes, and the pride of life. He had been close enough to Jesus to know that we are more than what we crave, what we possess, and what we can control. The immediacy of these is a pathway to anxiety and death. He knew Jesus well. He was loved by Him, and he loved Him in return.

I wandered through the house like Moses in the Horeb wilderness, beaten down under the weight of all that had happened to get me where I was. After a few hours of unsuccessfully trying to settle myself down, I convinced myself that the best course of action was distraction. I didn't have the self-awareness or the emotional energy to see things with any sense of clarity in the moment. I was primal, operating in a mode of subsistence. I needed something to take my mind off the immediate weight of it all. Something menial and tangible. I had often heard it said that people who work with their hearts need a steady diet of working with their hands. My heart was overworked and needed to be offset, or so I thought.

I remembered that we had made plans for Ashley's brother, Reid, and his family to spend a few days with us over the coming Christmas holiday. We were starving for familiar community, for laughter around the table. The kind of people who, with one look, can tell what you're thinking. Eleven22 was our new church community, but we didn't have the luxury of years of common experience to draw upon there yet. I had no doubt that it was available, but we couldn't begin that process. Not yet. The thought of sharing meaningful days with family in our

Jacksonville house brought a sense of comfort to us. It's what we needed, but we were ashamed of the state of the house itself. We were a long way from the charm of the red room at Westdel Bourne. Ashley's family had a long, successful track record of creating environments in which to live and thrive. It's one of the things I love about them. We needed a lot of time to create that in Jacksonville. But we needed family more.

When the decision was made to host Reid's family, we had come up with a preliminary plan for sleeping arrangements. We would give their family full reign of the second floor. There were two bedrooms and a full bathroom that would accommodate their needs. Of the many things that required attention in the house, the second-floor bathroom was near the top of the list of offenders. Layers of garish wallpaper and the flamboyant lime green marble countertop were adding to the tightness in my chest. I pulled Ashley aside and tried to share how I was feeling with her. I still remember the conversation. "Babe . . . I don't know how to say this, but . . . I feel like I'm losing my mind. If I don't do something good with my hands, I might fall off the deep end." She knew I was in a war, desperate for some way out of the foxhole.

Looking back, I can see that a big part of what motivated me was pride. I couldn't stand the thought of my brother-in-law brushing his teeth at the sink up there. Not with that countertop. I had constructed a scenario in my head that I knew wasn't real. In the midst of all I was carrying, I imagined him putting his toothbrush down in disgust, saying, "What is with this place? How can my sister live like this?" Reid Greven, the real Reid Greven, would never say something like this, but I wasn't in the frame of mind to convince myself otherwise. In fact, I am not entirely sure my mind had any sense of frame at all.

Jesus said (in King James for effect), "For which of you, intending to build a tower, sitteth not down first, and counteth the cost, whether he have sufficient to finish it? Lest haply, after he hath laid the foundation, and is not able to finish it, all that behold it begin to mock him, saying, This man began to build, and was not able to finish" (Luke 14:28-30, KJV). What a brilliant observation of the human condition. I'd like to think that attempted therapeutic bathroom remodels are inferred in the original language. In absolute haste, I walked up the stairs and turned the corner toward the bathroom. I had no tools, no detailed plans. All I had was an anxious heart and a divided mind. I didn't even want to take the time to acknowledge the scope of the work that needed to be done. I just wanted to do it. Something. Anything.

I walked into the bathroom and immediately flung open the doors to the builder-grade vanity that was holding up the lime green countertop. I grabbed the rigid metal handles of the shut-off valves for both the hot and cold-water lines and cranked them counterclockwise as far as they would go. With my bare hands, I began to unscrew the undercarriage of the kitschy faucet that sat atop the countertop. When the wingnuts securing the faucet had been fully removed, I jerked the faucet up triumphantly from the countertop, leaving a gaping hole where it used to be. I threw the faucet behind me haphazardly. It landed with a metallic *clank* as it collided with the cheap vinyl flooring. I reached hurriedly for the lime green backsplash that sat behind. It had to go. My fingers twitched as I tried to find a place to grab hold. My lack of options frustrated me.

After a few minutes of pulling with no success, I trudged down the stairs to the garage, threw open the toolbox, and grabbed the biggest flathead screwdriver I could find. I looked at it with pride. My pace quickened as I climbed back up the stairs. Chemicals were released in my brain as I punctured the drywall above the lime green backsplash and began to pry it away from the wall with the screwdriver. Progress. With the backsplash now in hand, I began to feel a slight sense of ease in my gut. I was operating in such a shallow manner that I didn't recognize what it was. It was the illusion of power. It illuminated things just enough for me to convince myself that I was in control. I was taking action. Things needed to be fixed, and I was doing it.

I took the screwdriver to the countertop itself, abruptly yanking it away from the vanity. My lower back flexed and stiffened as I twisted myself out of the door, bearing the weight of the marble slab in front of me. I strained around the corner and back down the stairs with successive thuds before squeezing through the door to the garage. As I let it drop on the garage cement floor, small shards of green marble splintered away upon impact. I took it as an act of triumph; the great green dragon had been slayed. I was King Arthur, wielding my flathead screwdriver like Excalibur. My heart rate spiked from carrying the countertop down the stairs, and sweat began to drip from the top of my head. But this was no time for rest and reflection; I couldn't let myself slow down.

After a few deep breaths, I pounced back up the stairs, taking three steps at a time. I made short work of the quarter round that surrounded the vanity kickplate. Now all that remained was the vanity itself. I took hold of it with my hands and attempted to use brute force to pull it away from the wall. With a quick upward jolt, I asserted myself on it. It didn't budge. I threw the cabinet doors open again, looking for the right place to grab. Digging my feet in like a stubborn dog, I heaved backward, mustering as much torque as I could. It was immovable, a stalwart. I was in a grudge match, and my ego would not accept defeat. In a moment of clarity, I peeked over the top edge of the cabinet. I saw four shiny bolts securing the cabinet to the studs behind the drywall. I immediately recognized it as an opportunity to employ the use of power tools. These are tools that increase one's sense of power. *Perfect*, I thought. I went back down to the garage and set the screwdriver down in the toolbox. It was time to move on to bigger and better things. Seconds later, I was pulling the trigger on my Dewalt screw gun like it was a .38 special. With each rev of the motor, my ambition surged.

I bent down over the open top of the cabinet and took the screw gun to the four bolts. They surrounded a six-inch hole in the back of the vanity that allowed the hot and cold water lines to pass through from behind the drywall, standard quarter-inch PVC pipes with the valves that I had previously shut off affixed to each end. As I backed out each bolt, I could feel the vanity begin to loosen from the

package. The inferno of rage followed, overtaking me as I sat up in bed screaming at Ashley. It made me feel like my dad. I hadn't yet thrown the rock on the Galilee shore. The Montana sunrise hadn't illuminated the Eno hammock, and the neck of the Gibson had yet to be snapped. I was still trapped in the vicious cycle of generational unforgiveness. I was carrying the sight of our friends waving goodbye in the rain in my rearview mirror as we pulled away from the Phoenix house. The loneliness that overtook Ashley and me in the living room in Jacksonville. The hurricane. The blue tarp. The sound of my mom's voice on the phone telling me that Daddy had died, and the sight of his body as it lay in the casket in Chicago.

I subconsciously channeled it all from my broken heart down into my fingers as I took hold of the vanity one last time. The veins on my hands popped as my grip tightened. I took a deep breath, closed my eyes, and in one blind act of aggression, I heaved backward. I pried the vanity away from the wall with my bare hands.

Pride and vanity.

> *The words of the Preacher, the son of David, king in Jerusalem. Vanity of vanities, says the Preacher, vanity of vanities! All is vanity. What does man gain by all the toil at which he toils under the sun? A generation goes, and a generation comes, but the earth remains forever.* (Ecclesiastes 1:1-4)

I heard a snap as I toppled back. Cold and hot water shot out of the wall like Old Faithful, pinning me to the opposing wall. The spray made it difficult for me to open my eyes to see what had happened. What had I done? I let go of the vanity and brought my hands to my face to shield my eyes. I saw the hot and cold water valves lying on the floor. Above them, the splintered PVC lines were bilging water at an alarming rate. The force I had put on the vanity had broken the pipes. My heart rate spiked. Whatever adrenaline lull my body had previously been capitalizing on had come to a sudden and abrupt end. My hands began to shake as I yelled over the rage of the water for help. Ashley shot up the stairs to see what had happened. For a moment, we were both completely paralyzed. She snapped out of it first and moved toward the broken pipes, attempting to stick her fingers in the ends to stop the flow. The water from the hot line scalded her finger. She instantly screamed and jerked her hand back. By this time, the entire bathroom and most of the hallway outside had been inundated. Devastation.

We devised a plan to divert the water to the adjacent bathtub while I ran to find another solution. I sprinted down the stairs to the garage and found an empty five-gallon bucket. Taking five steps at a time, I leaped back up the stairs and tossed the bucket to Ashley. She started to bail the water from the gushing pipes into the tub one bucketful at a time. It was all she could do. As I rushed back down the stairs, I looked to my left and began to see water pouring down from the ceiling of the first floor onto the wooden floor below. The power of gravity and water were at work, destroying the house.

I sprinted back into the garage and looked for a valve to shut off. The water heater, the water softener, none of them stopped the flow. I turned back into the house to grab my phone, hearing the water pouring from the ceiling as I entered. Running into the kitchen, my feet splashed in two inches of standing water that had collected on the floor below. My fingers twitched as I tried to find a number for a local plumber. I didn't know what else to do. After locating one, I pressed the green call button and held the phone up to my ear. When the call was answered, the volume of my voice shot up as I tried to explain what was happening. I struggled to string the words together as my mind raced. The voice on the other end of the phone recognized the direness of the situation and tried to calm me down. They proceeded to guide me to the main water valve in the utility box where the driveway met the street.

The utility box had a heavy, rectangular cement cover on it. With the same intensity I had used to pry the vanity from the wall, I grabbed hold of it, attempting to pull it off. Seconds ticked away as I wrestled, knowing that each one that passed would lead to more damage. After finding a handhold, I heaved upward on the cover and threw it aside. My eyes darted downward to find the shut-off valve. The box was filled to the brim with jet black loose dirt. I dropped to my knees and dug away at the dirt with my hands, tossing it up in the air. I was frantic.

After a minute or so of excavation, I located the valve. I tried to rotate it by hand, gripping as hard as I could. My hands, wet from the burst of water, couldn't find traction. I ran into the garage and threw the lid of my toolbox open, looking for some way to improvise. There was the screwdriver. I quickly grabbed it and the adjustable crescent wrench that lay beside it. In as short a time as I could manage, I fitted the crescent wrench to the crossbar atop the valve with the butt of the wrench jutting upward out of the box. Threading the screwdriver through the hole at the end of the wrench to form a T, I pulled counterclockwise and felt the valve shift. The sound of rushing water came to a halt.

I sprawled out flat on my back on the driveway for a moment and tried to calm myself down. The bright blue Florida sky hovered overhead, the sunshine beaming down on my exhausted body. I felt insulted by it, as if the sun had no regard for what I had just experienced. It was silent and unmoved. I was broken and living in the illusion that I was the middle of it all. Pre-Copernican. My world was underwater, drowning in chaos, but it didn't seem to bother the sun much. My clothes were caked with rich mud. My face bore a resemblance to William Wallace before the attack on Longshanks at Falkirk, but I was no hero. I was no victim either. The bright blue Florida sky owed me nothing. The blame was mine, and my shoulders slouched under its weight.

I struggled to sit up. After pushing myself off the ground, I walked slowly toward the front door of the house. My shoes made a gentle sloshing noise with each progressive step. Upon entrance, I was confronted with the reality that I had created. Water fell like steady rain from the ceiling. It drizzled down the tawdry brass chandelier over the dining room table as it made its way downward, each drop adding to the pooling now inches deep below. It was seeping down through the seams of the hardwood floor.

I looked to the left and saw Ashley, soaking wet. She was breathing heavily from her work with the bucket. We met at the bottom of the stairs. Our eyes locked as we stood silently in utter disbelief. Her face was still, and her eyes had a vacant stare, unable to process what was happening around her. It was as if she had been confronted by some strange apparition that had reached down into her gut and pulled her zest for life away. After a beat, her eyes pulled away from mine as she turned to survey the damage that surrounded us. Everything was in complete disarray. Any sense of the safety and security of home was being eroded by the falling water. A split second later, her eye sockets jutted to their open-most position, and the jugular vein on her neck bulged. Her vacant stare was overtaken by extreme emotion. She shrieked, "The piano!"

My neck careened to the right. I saw what she saw. There sat the Heintzman against the front room wall adjacent to the large bay window, situated directly under the bathroom above. It was uncanny, almost as if it had been placed strategically in the path that would afford it the most destruction. It had borne the brunt of the deluge from the burst pipes and was completely drenched. Water continued to pummel it from what had collected on the bathroom floor upstairs. I darted toward the piano and grabbed it by the front leg and back handle. In a last-ditch surge of Hulk-like strength, I flung the piano away from the wall. Its century-old wheels squealed as they glided across the floor toward the center of the room, creating a wake that rippled behind. I glanced back at Ashley. Her eyes, now jolted from their vacancy, began to betray the trouble in her heart. Tears amassed in the corners. They began to flow down her cheeks in concert with the water that dripped from the ceiling. Moving toward her, I reached out my arms. We stood there together in the front room and embraced one another in the middle of it all. Just as the most unlikely rain had fallen in the desert upon our departure weeks before, so an unlikely rain met us on the other side of the country, under our own roof. There was nothing to say, no way to acknowledge verbally the weight of how this accentuated the season in which we found ourselves. We were alone and in grief, drenched in both water and tears.

We pulled two chairs out from the dining room table and sat down on the waterlogged upholstery that covered the seats. It began to dawn on us that we had lost track of our children in the frenzy. Ashley called out for Brody, who answered immediately. Beckett was still immobile at the time. He had been taking in the show from his baby chair around the corner in the kitchen. Two of the three had been accounted for. It took us a while to track down our middle, Bentley. He was just out of the toddler phase and had the tendency and the ability to wander. Our neighbors, the Waldrons, whom we had never met, saw him walk out the front door by himself. They saw my frantic preoccupation with the valve at the street and knew we were dealing with a code red situation. They took him in, made him a peanut butter and jelly sandwich, and sat him down in front of the TV to watch Mickey Mouse Clubhouse. They also proactively called ServePro, who, unbeknownst to us, had dispatched a unit to begin the process of cleaning up the water and drying out the house. It was a most peculiar way for one to make the acquaintance of new neighbors. But it took. It's since become a staple tale in the neighborhood lore.

With all our children accounted for, we took to the task of observing the fallout on a more detailed level. Ashley hesitantly made her way over to the Heintzman. Of all that had been damaged, it was the thing that she cared about the most. In the strange new world we now lived in, it was a window into a sense of the familiar. Not just the familiar, but of family itself. It conjured up welcomed memories of her mother as a little girl shaping simple chords with her cold fingers in the frigid Chatham garage. A generation later, her brother was doing the same with shoulders aglow under the subtle Westdel Borne skylight. The sound of the piano resonating in the red room as Dave spoke his native tongue on the bench could still faintly be heard in our memory. Its sound was so instrumental to the sense of the common union of worship amongst the people closest to us at the celebratory feast before our wedding vows. It was so much more than wood, ivory, and brass in the same way we are so much more than flesh and bone. It evoked a sense of connection to something deeper, to legacy and to home.

Ashley placed her bare palm atop the wooden cabinet and wiped away the water that had collected on the murky walnut finish. Her fingers drifted downward to the keys below. I stood behind her and watched as she pressed down on the keys. The once vibrant resonance of the giant brass soundboard, as the felt hammers struck the old steel strings, had been replaced by a series of muffled thuds. The deadness of each successive thud echoed through the chamber of the piano with the same eerie sense of space the notes had had minutes before. She moved up and down the keyboard, hoping to find some sign of life, some sense of breath. The keys dropped like frontline infantry soldiers in a civil war battle. Each fell like a dead man to the damp battleground below. Her heart sank with them. Few gave off a faint sense of tonality, barely enough to distinguish one note from the next. They were the mortally wounded. Most completely lifeless like corpses, devoid of spirit or personality, lying in the walnut casket that surrounded them. The Heintzman, once an instrument animated in joyful expression, had become a silent and dark tomb.

By the time ServePro arrived, most of the water had made its way to the first floor. They descended on the mess in force. There were shop vacs, industrial fans, and dehumidifiers by what seemed to be the dozens. Men in brightly colored uniforms crept along the interior walls of the house with space-age moisture detectors sniffing out the potential for mold. This was Florida, and humid air was job security. They were highly skilled and highly compensated surgeons deciding what parts of the drywall were cancerous and needed to be removed. In a few short hours, they had eradicated the standing water, carted off the soaked floor coverings for cleaning, and left us with an extremely ambiguous piece of paper outlining the financial ramifications of the work that had been done. The parallels in the process to the confusion of the US healthcare system were startling.

As we deciphered the invoice, we saw that we were to be charged an hourly rate for each dehumidifier and fan in use, in addition to the labor costs for removing the damaged drywall and the water itself. Dollar signs were growing exponentially as the house dried out. For a moment, I reeled with PTSD from my experience with the hurricane. I remembered my battle with the Cosa Nostra. I also remembered John Longfellow, the inside man. Without hesitation, I scrolled down my contacts to his number. When he answered my call, I stepped outside. The overall decibel level in the house from all the machinery at work rose so high that one could hardly make out what the other was saying in face-to-face conversation, let alone over the phone. I tried to describe all that had transpired. I could tell that he was having a hard time believing it from the tone of his voice on the other end of the line. By the end of the conversation, an appointment had been scheduled for John to return to the house and assess the damage.

As the afternoon turned into evening, Ashley and I noticed the internal temperature. The fans that ServePro had installed were billowing with heat. The front room of the house started to feel like Phoenix in the dead of summer. The heat rose to the second floor, pushing the upstairs thermostat to its peak reading of ninety-nine degrees. Its digital screen lacked the ability to move into the triple digits. The only reprieve in the house could be found in our bedroom. It was tucked around the right side of the house, removed from the fallout of the bathroom above. We decided that the only course of action was for all of us to spend the night together in our room.

Chapter 14

Ashley presented the idea to the boys in a spirit of adventure. It would be like a slumber party or an indoor camping trip. The chaos of the day was so jarring to them that they couldn't decide how to react. As the sun began to set, we collected a pack n' play, two mattresses, and sleeping bags from the boy's bedrooms upstairs and situated them like puzzle pieces on our bedroom floor. Ashley's maternal instincts kicked in, situating pillows and blankets in a way that would make everyone as comfortable as possible.

A few hours after the sun went down, each of the kids drifted off to sleep, one by one, releasing themselves from the cares of the day. The fans hummed like a giant white noise machine behind the closed double doors, and the air conditioning blew icy cold as the thermostat compensated for the rising temperatures on the other side. The tempest on the other side. Ashley and I lay silently in bed staring up at the ceiling. Partly because we were trying not to wake the boys, but mostly because we didn't know what else to do. Ashley's leg crossed the middle of the bed and made contact with mine. Her touch, her presence, brought a softness to my spirit. It warmed my body.

> *Two are better than one, because they have a good reward for their toil. For if they fall, one will lift up his fellow. But woe to him who is alone when he falls and has not another to lift him up! Again, if two lie together, they keep warm, but how can one keep warm alone? And though a man might prevail against one who is alone, two will withstand him—a*

threefold cord is not quickly broken.

(Ecclesiastes 4:9-12)

We had experienced so much heartbreak. We had weathered it together, side by side. When I overreacted in the deficit of my own grief, she chose not to stop me. When the pipes burst and the damage had been done, she decided to bail with a bucket, and I dug with my hands. There was no hint of finger-pointing. In a show of beautiful selflessness, Ashley had forfeited her opportunity to leverage the events of the day toward heaping burning coals of blame upon my head. She had experienced an immense amount of loss just as I had. I saw her demeanor drop as she stood over the Heintzman. I knew the warm recesses of her tender heart that were under assault as she heard the thud pressing down on the keys. In a show of silent protest to all that could divide, our hands locked under the soft white duvet cover. We lay motionless on our backs under the gentle whir of the ceiling fan above. The heaviness of our limbs pulled us under, and we lay comatose in parallel lines.

CHAPTER 15

At the point at which we find ourselves in the story, I'm hesitant to include what happened next. To be completely honest, I can't quite bring myself to believe that it happened. But it did. In the Author's Note of this book, I offered commentary on the nature of *true* story, particularly how it stands in contrast to fiction. The heart behind that commentary is this: Truth deals in realities. Fiction has a way of packaging truth up in a preferred outcome and tying a bow on it for good measure. Truth is elemental. If fiction is a gourmet meal, truth is the key ingredient stacked up in the pantry. The real stuff.

As hard as it is to believe, and as difficult as it is to recount, the *truth* is that the Olsons didn't drift off into euphoria that night. And there was no blissful sense of brand new that awaited us on the flip side of the next sunrise. The truth is that a few short hours after Ashley and I drifted off hand in hand, a ghastly sound abruptly awoke us from the area where Brody, our eldest son, was sleeping. Ashley and I shot out of bed and turned the lights on to see what had happened. Brody was violently vomiting in the bed that we made for him. His little body was convulsing as he worked through it. Ashley instantly moved into clean-up mode. Blankets and pajamas were carted off. The double doors shot open, letting the Gehenna heat and the raucous noise of the fans cascade into our bastion of peace. She dragged the vomit-covered linens to the laundry room and scraped them into the utility sink before piling them in the washing machine. She cranked the dial to the sterilize setting. Copious amounts of towels and a large stainless-steel bowl were laid gently around Brody in anticipation of a repeat episode. Ashley pressed the back of her hand against Brody's forehead. It was moist with perspiration and warm with fever. It was only the beginning.

Over the course of the next twelve hours, in precise four-hour increments, our entire family succumbed to one of the most mutant, contagious twenty-four-hour stomach viruses in the history of our family. Ashley was next in line. Her proximity to Brody in his time of need found a weak spot in her immune system. She was Mother Theresa living amongst the lepers, the picture of mercy. But in the middle of the night, she dragged herself to the bathroom and began her shift. She groaned as she trekked back and forth from the bed to the bathroom as the virus ran its course. I tried to comfort her, but necessity snapped me to attention, taking her place in Brody's aid, emptying and rinsing bowls and changing towels.

Chapter 15

After each occurrence, I recklessly scrubbed my hands to avoid the inevitable. Then, a little less than eight hours in and with two of us already down, little Beckett chimed in. Ashley lunged from the bed to attend to him, but she was too weak. I calmed him down, changed his tiny powder blue jammies, and doused the pack 'n play with a cloud of Lysol before laying him back down to sleep on a new blanket. Bentley was next. He followed in the same pattern, lying a few feet from his older brother. The two shared the large stainless-steel bowl that lay between them. I would follow shortly behind. By the time all was said and done, we had worked through every bath towel and bowl we owned. We had been hijacked. Our cozy indoor family camping trip turned into a wartime infirmary. The room was filled with moans and groans, aches, and pains. Water glasses, Gatorade bottles, and the small cups and syringes used to administer Tylenol and Motrin to small children began to pile on the surface of our bedside tables. None of us proved to be immune.

By mid-morning the next day, I found myself wild with fever, lying prostrate on Miss Robin's emerald green ceramic tile in the guest bathroom just outside the double doors. The bathroom door was open, allowing the noise and heat in. I pressed whatever bare skin I could manage against the tile to cool myself down. In minute-to-minute cycles, my body bounced between extremes. One second, giant goose bumps were shooting up off the surface of my skin like icebergs on my arms; the next, those same arms were beading up with burning sweat. My head was spinning. My legs were cramping. The fans and dehumidifiers, just around the corner, added to the dehydration. I lay there on the floor, trying to find the balance between mustering the fortitude to push through the virus on my own and staying present with the empathy needed to care for the rest of my family. I couldn't do it . . . literally . . . physically. I had reached the limit. I was unable.

A different version of the spirit of helplessness crept over me than when the pipes broke after I yanked the vanity away from the wall. It moved in like a shadow, ominous and dark. In dealing with all that I had been carrying up until that point, I had been fighting the battles of the mind, taking thoughts captive. Now I realized I didn't even have the strength to pick myself up off the bathroom floor. I was sick and I lacked the ability to heal myself. I was beyond myself. Mortal. Finite. It wasn't that I hadn't fallen ill before; I certainly had many times. But I had to consider the context, and there had been a lot of it, all at once. I had been abruptly and forcefully awoken from my Superman dream. There was a common theme, a devastatingly beautiful strand of truth that was rising to the surface. God was *speaking*. What was He saying? Nothing that He hadn't said before. The words were given in equal amounts of sternness and affection, grace, and truth.

> *Shall a faultfinder contend with the Almighty? He who argues with God, let him answer it. Then Job answered the Lord and said: "Behold, I am of small account; what shall I answer you? I lay my hand on my mouth. I have spoken once, and I will not answer; twice, but I will proceed no further." Then*

the Lord answered Job out of the whirlwind and said: "Dress for action like a man; I will question you, and you make it known to me. Will you even put me in the wrong? Will you condemn me that you may be in the right? Have you an arm like God, and can you thunder with a voice like his? Adorn yourself with majesty and dignity; clothe yourself with glory and splendor. Pour out the overflowings of your anger, and look on everyone who is proud and abase him. Look on everyone who is proud and bring him low and tread down the wicked where they stand. Hide them all in the dust together; bind their faces in the world below. Then will I also acknowledge to you that your own right hand can save you.

(Job 40:1-14)

It's hard to understand. It's even harder to describe. But there is a beautiful grace that can only be discovered when you find yourself crushed down under the heavy weight of God's glorious arm of disciplinary love. It is paradoxical. He is a gentleman and yet a warrior. A lion, and yet a lamb. In the most aggressive tenderness, you are brought to the mat. And with the precision and care of a master surgeon, he grabs your jaw and compels you to look him in the eye. And it is grace. You wriggle and writhe. Your attention and affections do all that they can to avoid the gravity of his fiery stare. But it's a pointless struggle. Eventually, the brutality of his lovingkindness will win you to your end. To the place where your feet can no longer find their own traction, where Job was. You cry out, *"Mercy!"* And He gives it to you. You are caught up in the Spirit, levitating in midair. You are beautifully broken and named anew. You see, there is death. It is dark, gruesome, and splintery like a Roman cross. But then there is something else. Something up a little further around the bend. It is unachieved and unmerited. Something breathtaking that would remain hidden from view if you hadn't been commandeered by the weight of His glory.

Ashley jumped back into caring for the family as soon as she came through the worst of it. She was angelic, appearing out of nowhere over my head as I lay on the bathroom floor with a bottle of bright orange Gatorade in one hand and a cold washcloth in the other. Mother Theresa. She embodied the purest grace and the sincerest compassion. I remembered that we had been united in Jesus's name. Dave led us in our vows. The words we used were "For better or for worse, in sickness or in health." Here we were.

John Longfellow showed up at the front door a few days later. His eyes popped in astonishment as he walked in. The blue tarp he had addressed weeks before still sat up on the roof waiting to be fixed. His work on that crisis was finished. But what could be made of what he saw inside? By that time, ServePro had removed a substantial amount of the damaged drywall, leaving the studs of the front room exposed. He raised his voice over the noise of the fans, "What happened?"

John's golf shirt embroidered with the company name might as well have been a priest's collar. The small, disheveled bathroom upstairs might as well have been a confessional booth. I pointed down to the capped PVC lines

I had snapped, describing what had happened. *Forgive me, Father Longfellow, for I have sinned.*

I didn't say the words, but that was the spirit of it. I owned it. I told him about my dad's funeral and the darkness that hit me. About the conversation with Ashley after I returned home. I re-enacted the scene of the crime, showing him how I had taken hold of the vanity and heaved it away from the wall. He wrote the details down on his legal pad as he listened. We walked back down the stairs to the front room. I showed him the Heintzman. The keys were exposed as the lid was opened, many of them still flattened to the surface below. I reached down and took my hand to the keyboard. *Thud, thud, thud.* John continued to write. After about twenty minutes, he had seen all that there was to see. He told us he would be in touch and walked out the front door.

Over the next few days, the house dried out, and we rehydrated from the virus. All five of us continued to go about our normal routines of work and school amidst the bare studs and warping wooden floors. It was a tasteful addition to the peeling wallpaper. The fans and dehumidifiers were removed in stages, lowering the overall temperature and decibel level. Eventually, the kids slept in their bedrooms.

John jumped into negotiations with our insurance company much like he did with the roof. I'm sure they were just as surprised as he was that the Olson home was back under the microscope. I wasn't there when he presented our case, but I would have loved to have been a fly on the wall. It was the notes on John's legal pad against the will of the Cosa Nostra number crunchers. Father Longfellow won the day. The insurance company couldn't prove any ill motivation in my attempt to remodel the bathroom. It was, in fact, pure stupidity operating under the banner of God's sovereign grace.

Providentially, the company that John had lined up for the roof replacement also specialized in home renovations. They were a one-stop shop. John walked the general contractor and me through the disheveled house as the three of us discussed the scope of the renovations per the agreement with the insurance company. An x amount of dollars for labor: plumbers, electricians, tile workers, drywall guys. And x amount of dollars for materials, including floors, fixtures, drywall, paint, crown molding, and a new vanity (which one stung a bit). John worked it all out on his legal pad and transferred it to a more formal-looking white paper agreement. The general contractor looked down at the agreement, pursed his lips, scratched his head, and said, "Three weeks." I looked at John and said, "Ok, so we'll start in three weeks." The contractor hiked up his pants. "No, we'll start in a week. But we'll need the house for three weeks."

By this time, all the panic had been drained out of my system. I didn't have much adrenaline left to expend on small details. I went with the flow and said, "Okay." After the contractor walked out of the house, John pulled Ashley and me over to the kitchen table and laid out the details on the money that had been negotiated for our living expenses during the renovation. There would be a certain amount of dollars per day for lodging, food, etc. In seven days, a team of tradesmen would swarm our house like locusts on a harvest time field. Shingles would be torn off, floors ripped up, and insulation pulled out. I had visions of myself playing the part of Tom Hanks in the movie *Money Pit*, rolling around in the back of my brain. Eccentric construction workers were climbing out of vehicles in the front driveway like circus clowns out of a Smart car as I stood at the front door. Collapsing staircases and booby-trap holes on the second-story floor were covered up by large Persian rugs. Tom lived in the house while it all went down. We didn't have much time to figure out where we were going to go. We had stuff to figure out.

That night, after the kids were down, Ashley and I moved into research mode. We poked around the internet looking for rates at extended-stay hotels that would be convenient to our school and work rhythms. I crunched the numbers. They weren't generous, and the clock was ticking. We both crawled into bed and held hands like we had the night the plague hit. This time, we asked for help. "God, we feel a little like Mary and Joseph headed to Bethlehem here . . . is there a stable somewhere nearby?" There was no audible reply, but we felt as though He had heard us. We fell asleep.

CHAPTER 16

The next morning, I made the short three-mile drive from our home to Eleven22. I pulled up in front of the old Walmart that the church had retrofitted into a worship space. At that time, the staff was much smaller in number than it is today. A large percentage of the forty or so full-time employees had a meeting to discuss matters pertaining to church life: weekend services, baptisms, care team, etc. I couldn't focus. All I could think about was avoiding the *Money Pit* scenario. Where were we going to sleep? Pastor Joby closed the meeting in prayer, grabbed a folding chair, and pulled it up to the round Rubbermaid portable table where I sat. He knew what we were wading through. Not just the house either . . . the desert, my dad, the hurricane. He gently asked how we were coming along with things. "Well . . . ," I told him about the events of the previous day. About John Longfellow and the contractor, the Cosa Nostra, the hotel search, and the ticking clock. He could see the fatigue in my face. With zero hesitation, he sat straight up in the folding chair and said, “Bro, you should just come stay with us.”

Some may be familiar with the acronym DTR. It’s not used a lot, but most commonly heard in the dating scene, a place where I (gratefully) have not been for a long time. It stands for Determine The Relationship. One of the things this story vividly illustrates is that relationships can be complicated, whether it’s between fathers and sons or friends who are like brothers. They all deal in the deep complexities of what makes us human. In fact, the more intimate the relationship, the more complicated it can become. Eventually, all relationships reach a point where clarity is needed. The questions to ask are: “Ok, what are we doing here? Where is this thing going?”

At this point, I had known Joby Martin for a grand total of four months. During this time, all hell had broken loose in our lives. Some pipes had too. The Olsons were a hot mess, all five of us, from dirty diapers and destructive toddlers to near nervous breakdowns. We were a three-ring circus. “Stay with us,” he said. It takes a unique kind of person to embrace that kind of mess, not just address it from behind a pulpit. But invite it into your home, where you sleep . . . without checking first with your wife. The truth is, Joby is so tunnel-visioned on what we call *the gospel* that it compels him to do unconventional things. What he was proposing was an extreme version of the DTR. It was the kind of thing that Jesus did to Zacchaeus when he saw him perched high up in the sycamore tree. "I'm comin' over!"

Ashley and I didn't know how to take it. Honestly, we didn't believe the invitation was legitimate. "Surely Gretchen will shut this down," we said as the clock continued to tick away. It never happened. She doubled down on us like a card shark in Vegas. Their doors remained wide open to us. Over a few late nights around our kitchen table, Ashley and I weighed our options. By that I mean, we realized we didn't have options. It became glaringly obvious that the Olsons moving in with the Martins was the best (and only) option. As the preparations were being made for the demolition of our place, we packed up for our grand adventure with Joby, Gretchen, JP, and Reagan.

A few days later, we piled in the front door of their house with four random pieces of road-worn luggage from my touring days, two diaper bags stuffed full of Huggies and butt paste, and a ratted-out pack n' play for Beckett that had been beaten to death by his two older brothers. We were greeted with heartfelt smiles and a "welcome home." The Martin home was modest and clean. There was a small collection of shoes and boots that sat just off the entrance to the house from the garage. Each one was neatly matched with its pair, and each pair had its own place specific to each member of the family. It was decorated with a tastefully eclectic collection of modern farmhouse pieces and assorted taxidermy. Artsy family pictures adorned the walls throughout, portraying the strong family value within. The light that filtered through the home was warm and welcoming, especially in the evening hours when the daylight gave way to the glow emanating from the lampshades placed strategically throughout the first floor. There was a sense of sound logic to the way the furniture was laid out. The dining room table was surrounded by more chairs than they needed for their family of four. The living room had a comfortably worn matching set of sofa and chairs that faced each other conversationally. I could tell that their life had been geared toward leveraging their home for meaningful relationship building. Meals and meaningful conversation. I walked through the kitchen on the way to the living room and peeked through the cracked pantry door. There were matching Tupperware bins evenly spaced on the shelves. Each one was individually labeled and organized by snack category. It had a librarian appeal to it. The house felt quiet and safe, standing in stark contrast to the chaos we had been living in just a few minutes up the road.

Just behind the shoes at the door to the garage was a secluded staircase that led up to the second floor. Joby and Gretchen each grabbed a suitcase, toting our belongings up the narrow staircase. I did my best to avoid making contact with the paint on the walls on the way up. There was an open door at the top that welcomed us into a small loft with an ensuite bath. After all the bags had been brought up, they politely left us to ourselves to get situated. The loft had two twin beds, each with a matching plush, bright red duvet cover and pillows. We decided to push the beds together to leave plenty of space on the floor for the older boys' sleeping bags. The loft had a large closet that we turned into Beckett's nursery. It was just big enough for the pack n' play to fit lengthwise across the back. We cracked open our suitcases, setting them out of the way as much as we could, and organized the kids' folded clothes in adjoining piles. Our toiletry bags were stowed on the floor of the bathroom just beneath the white pedestal sink.

After a few moments of settling in, we were summoned to a family meeting. We walked down the narrow staircase and made a right turn through the hallway, lined with photos, leading to the open living room. The four Martins stood in the room's center. Joby, the elder statesman of the family, proceeded to open his arms and give the official welcome. It was a "Mi Casa, Su Casa" sermon. It was informal, but it was anything but a formality. The main point was biblical generosity and care lived out in the most practical of forms. Jesus in clean sheets and towels, chairs around breakfast tables, refrigerator rights, and late-night conversations over prerecorded Braves games on the back patio. It became clear that our inability to afford the extended stay was, in fact, an open door to what we really needed, a connection to the body of Christ.

Over the next three weeks, we lived it out. Babies cried in the night, messes were made and cleaned up, the Olson boys pilfered the pantry, at least the ones who could walk. JP Martin, who was five years older than Brody, became a folk hero to them. He immediately garnered that mysterious and instantaneous respect that materializes out of the ether when young boys encounter an older and wiser version of themselves. They gravitated toward his bedroom, which was filled with new and fascinating things like Nerf guns and posters of famous athletes with magnetic force. Ashley became a surrogate gymnastics coach for Reagan. Her previous experience as a tumble coach in our Nashville days proved to be a valuable asset. The main hallway of the house transformed into a tumble track where tips and tricks for successful back handsprings were fleshed out in real time. Reagan would flip her heels over her head as Ashley knelt and supported her arching back with her open palm.

Most nights, after we put the kids to bed, the four adults would find themselves down in the living room. The kind of casual, spontaneous conversations that break out in the course of everyday life would pop up. Parenting challenges, the funny things that kids do or say, and peculiar things that are noticed around the neighborhood. There was comfort in it for Ashley and me. We were in someone else's home, but we weren't strangers. We didn't have years of equity and experience with Joby and Gretchen, but it didn't seem to matter. They weren't guarding themselves from us. As the evenings would drift into the later hours, Ashley and Gretchen would retire, leaving Joby and me to ourselves.

On a few occasions, the conversation would shift to the people that we were now shepherding together, with me under his leadership. I had been there for a matter of months. He had been in the trenches with these people since the church's inception. Some of them before that. People with names and faces who were in the middle of health concerns, marital issues, and financial crises. Lost jobs, prodigal children, and the deep wounds that infidelity inflicts on the peace of a home. I resonated with it. The tone and volume of our voices hushed with subtlety and reverence as we acknowledged the needs.

One particular evening, the conversation was more intense than the others had been. It carried on well into the night. The living room was mostly dark as all the lamps had been switched off by our wives when they went to bed. There was a faint light filtering over our shoulders from the kitchen behind us. I could see the outline of Joby's facial features as we talked. The intense eyes that I first looked into across the table at Angie's subs when I first visited Eleven22 became windows into the deep internal work of pastoral care. The unquantifiable heaviness that comes with seeing people walk through the valley of the shadow and offering the compassionate heart of Jesus along the way. I was struck by the sobriety in his voice. Words were few, but they were well chosen. I was tired. Ashamed to admit it, my eyelids became too heavy for me to bear. As the microwave clock pushed up to the midnight hour, there was a brief lull in the conversation. I acquiesced. I got up from the couch and made my way to the narrow staircase. Ashley had fallen asleep in the adjoining twin beds under the red duvet cover in the loft upstairs. As I approached the first step, I turned back and glanced through the kitchen. I saw Joby standing by himself, head bowed, bracing his hands on the back of a breakfast table chair. He was in prayer. It was silent to the ear, but I'm absolutely certain that there was a loud and raucous war being waged in the heavenly realm. I paused for a moment and observed him. This was the work of the shepherd.

Previously, I had seen this all approached so differently, yet it had been presented so convincingly. There were organizational charts and corporate alignment, as well as tips and tricks learned from fancy hotel chains on how to create more comfortable environments for parishioners. But this was a different gear. It was intercession and supplication. It was about seeing past the perceived needs that people have for themselves with spiritual eyes and claiming the finished work of Christ over their brokenness. Wielding the sword of the Spirit, the living word of God Himself, to the ends of seeing His kingdom advance in the hearts and lives of the people under your care. I turned toward the staircase. As I climbed the steps, I felt a sense of rest and gratitude for what I saw.

The next day, I met John Longfellow at the house. He continued negotiations with the insurance company regarding our claim. The scope of the damage and repair to the home had been settled. The only outlying negotiations that remained were over the personal belongings that had been lost in the flood. Most of the salvaged belongings were moved into the portable storage units, which sat in the driveway. When we walked through the front door, I was overcome by how vacant it felt. The construction crew had already begun to hang large swaths of plastic sheeting around the house in preparation for the impending demolition. There, in the middle of the front room covered in a polyethylene shroud, sat the lifeless Heintzman. John walked up to it and pulled the plastic away. The morning light shining through the large bay window highlighted the water damage on its exterior. They looked like scars. As he reached down into his bag for his legal pad, he broached the conversation, "Michael, the insurance company is trying to figure out how to handle this."

He expressed the insurance company's desire to take ownership of the piano and reimburse us for its appraised value. It was the most efficient way for them to address the situation. Big insurance companies thrive on efficiency. My heart shriveled as I envisioned it being loaded up into a white box truck by men who had no idea what it meant to us. It shriveled even more as I pictured myself with a $500 reimbursement check in my hand as the truck drove away. I opened the lid and pressed the keys. *Thud, thud, thud.* Images of the journey the piano had been on flooded through my mind. Goldy Reid, the Chatham house, and young Double G. Reid pelted by a wet washcloth from the kitchen of Westdel Bourne for his lack of focus. The sweet sound of worship in the red room, my dad on the bench in the Phoenix front room. I saw the look of panic on my wife's face when we realized it was beneath the bathroom. I tried again. *Thud, thud, thud.*

"John, I just don't think I can do it. What are our options?" I asked with curiosity. He glanced down at his legal pad and scratched his head. "Well, the only other option is to try to negotiate for its repair. But it would be complicated, and it probably won't work. We would need to know more about it and find an expert. Someone who could tell us what it's really worth, and what it would take to fix it."

I paused and considered what he said. In a moment, it became clear that what he had proposed was the only wall behind it. With the four bolts now lying on the cabinet floor, I was left with one remaining task. It would be the most fulfilling. I began to picture the large, vacant spot where the vanity, holding the lime-green countertop, used to lie. Something new would take its place. A new vanity, something less offensive to me, and to my brother-in-law.

In the moment, I didn't have the sense of presence to think about all that had transpired to bring me to that spot. In fact, I was trying to avoid thinking about it. One could argue that I was avoiding thinking altogether. But I couldn't escape it. It was with me, all of it. Strapped to my back like an anvil. I was carrying the Sunday morning memories of my mom and dad up at the front of Northwest under the colored sunlight from the fake stained glass. The beautiful sound that echoed through the A-frame from the organ as my dad swayed and played, and the fire that destroyed it. The site of the hymnal pages drafting up into the air off the intense heat of the smoldering church below, as I sat with Jimmy on the swings. I was carrying the dark anger that materialized out of nowhere, which led my dad into the captivity of despondency and isolation. I felt the heaviness in my mother's eyes as she waded neck deep through the mire of depression and shame. The light from the TV flashed from the living room as we sat in silent tension around the dinner table.

I was questioning how and why things were the way they were. The sharp tongue of a mega church pastor that maligned my sense of manhood. The wilderness of losing my closest friend to corporate alignment. The bistro table outside the coffee shop, where he offered the severance way forward. The Heintzman was not about bureaucratic efficiency with quick tit-for-tat transactions. It was about legacy. It was about beauty and spirit. We had lost so much. We needed to do everything possible to stay in the fight over this one.

That's when I met Fred. After a few conversations with co-workers and some brief phone calls, I discovered that Fred Brown was the obvious man for the job. He was the only Steinway-approved technician in North Florida. Fred oversaw the maintenance and care of all the pianos at the University of North Florida, a school known for its prestigious jazz program. He tuned them and reconditioned them. He had an obscure website that popped up a few pages into a Google search. It looked like it had been designed in the Stone Age of the World Wide Web. It had a section dedicated to pianos that he had refurbished, complete with photos of the process. The pictures were terrible, but the reconstructions themselves were impressive. After a few minutes, I found his number and called him. The phone rang a few times, and an airy, faint voice answered on the other side, "Hello?" After confirming that it was indeed Fred, I attempted to describe the situation in which I found myself, trying to avoid the unnecessary and complicated details. I talked about the flood and what John had said about the insurance company. I got the impression that Fred had seen similar situations in the past. He took an interest and agreed to come out the following day to take a closer look.

Fred pulled up to the Jacksonville house in an old, beat-up Toyota minivan. The kind that people buy for their practicality. I immediately recognized the wear and tear on it as being more the result of working in the trade than carting kids around. This was confirmed when he climbed out of the driver's side door. Fred was in his late fifties. He wore a business casual button-down shirt with a collar to present well to a potential client, but his jeans were old and faded. He was long and lanky, and his movements were slow and calculated, reminiscent of the giraffes I had seen at the zoo growing up as a kid. I watched him grab his old leather bag from the passenger seat and sling it over his shoulder through the windows by the front door. He sauntered past the storage units that had been dropped in the driveway and the dumpster that had arrived in preparation for the demolition day. I opened the door and greeted him with a handshake. His response was very mild-mannered. I could tell that his demeanor was not naturally inclined towards excitability. As we walked into the front room, he acknowledged the state it was in, "Must have been some accident." I couldn't deny it. I was ashamed to divulge all the gritty details that went into where and why things were the way they were.

The Heintzman sat alone in the front room like the proverbial elephant. Fred approached it with a steady gaze as he began his assessment. I could tell by the way he moved around the piano, the way he gestured toward it, that he had experience with instruments like this. I had spent years sitting at the bench creating. Shaping chords and melodies much like my father before me. Fred knew this instrument on a more intimate level. He not only knew what it could do, but how it could do it. He had spent decades studying the way it was made and how the intricacies of its internal mechanics worked in concert with one another in allowing someone like me to create on it.

I had assumed that Fred's first move would be to lift the lid and attempt to play the keys much like I had done. Instead, Fred pulled forward on the large rectangular walnut panel that sat just above the keys. He removed it completely, exposing the century-old felt-covered wooden hammers. Reaching into his bag, he grabbed an old pair of readers and perched them on the bridge of his nose as he sat on the bench. He moved his face as close as he could to the innards of the Heintzman. The closer he got, the more it dawned on me how complex the instrument was. It was purposefully designed by a master craftsman. The strings ran vertically from the floor to the top over a heavy brass soundboard that was bolted to the cabinet. Each felt-covered hammer was drawn by a slender woven piece of canvas-like fabric that acted as a connection to the corresponding keys, eighty-eight in all. Additionally, a series of dampers muted the strings when the various pedals were in use. Some for sustaining and some for softening the tone. The brass pedal system was connected to the long main damper bar by a series of long wooden dowel rods. The dark wood damper bar running across the length of the strings bore the same gold embossed mark as the bottom of the lid that covered the keys. *Heintzman*. It was beautifully sophisticated. I sat and watched Fred as he moved his nose up and down the system of hammers.

It was uncomfortably silent for a moment until his soft voice broke it. "This is a really nice piano," he remarked.

I looked at him quizzically. Fred continued, "It's North American-made, Toronto, built at the turn of the century. Heintzman was a highly reputable piano maker back then. The only thing I could compare it to would be an early 1900s upright Steinway Grand." I felt like a guest on *Antiques Roadshow*, sitting across from the expert as he examined my wares. My curiosity piqued as he continued, "In decent condition, this piano would be worth north of $20,000." My jaw dropped and my heart leapt simultaneously as I considered Ashley's grandfather, Goldy Reid, dropping off an instrument of that value at the Chatham house. How did he get it? Did he know what it was worth? Could Ashley's mom possibly have known what she was sitting in front of in that frigid garage after the fire in the house on the Thames River? The sense of legacy surrounding the Heintzman grew exponentially in my gut. Fred continued, "It's in really bad shape. All the action has been compromised. The glue holding the hammers together took a hit. The felt is ruined. The strings are pretty corroded, and the finish on the outside took on a good bit of water damage in the accident." I was still trying to process how much the piano was worth. Fred opened the lid, exposing the keys, and formed some chords. He was unfazed by the gentle thuds that followed as he pressed down.

Things started to catch up with me. I recalled my conversation with John Longfellow. Fred was the expert we were looking for. He had given an assessment. I realized that I needed to follow up with a very important question. "Can you fix it?" I asked. I was terrified of what he might say in response. Fred stood up from the bench, stepped back from the piano, and folded his readers in the palm of his right hand. His eyes worked their way over the Heintzman from bottom to top. He slowly moved behind the cabinet in his giraffe-like gate and pressed the palm of his hand against the water-damaged finish. "Yeah, I could fix it," he responded. "But it would take a complete rebuild. I'd have to gut the whole thing out and start from scratch. Replace the action and the strings. I'd have to strip the finish completely, sand it down, and start again on it."

I had no concept of the scope of what he was talking about, or how one would even begin a project like that. However, the steadiness in the delivery of his words and his calm demeanor led me to trust him. When I looked at the Heintzman, all I could see was the disaster that I had been so instrumental in creating. Fred Brown looked at the same thing and saw something completely different. He saw great value and potential, and he had the know-how and the tools to get the job done.

"Fred, how much would something like this cost?" I asked. Another pause. "Oh, somewhere in the neighborhood of $14,000, I suppose. That's pretty standard for a rebuild like this. It will be about a four to five-month process." It was another shock to the system. At this point, I can confidently say that Ashley and I hadn't owned a car worth that much money. I did my best to keep a poker face. "Fred, can you write all this down on a piece of paper?" I asked. "Sure," he replied. He reached down into his bag and pulled out a small pad of white carbon paper. The top of the paper read: "Fred Brown, Registered Piano Technician, Dedicated service in tuning, repair, and rebuilding since 1991." With the quick click of a ballpoint pen, he began to bullet point the prospective job. Toward the bottom of the page, the size of his handwriting grew to twice the size as he wrote the number $14,000.00. He circled it for added emphasis. He clicked the pen again, slid it into the pocket of his collared shirt, and ripped the top copy of the carbon paper with a quick tug.

As we walked back toward the front door, he handed the paper to me, mentioning, "Let me know what they say." His eyes briefly made contact with mine. Then Fred slowly walked back down the driveway past the dumpster and storage units to the old minivan. He opened the driver's side door and crammed his long legs in one at a time. After a few seconds of struggle, the engine turned over. He pulled around the cul-de-sac and out of sight. As the engine sound disappeared, I stood in the front room next to the Heintzman with the white piece of carbon paper in hand. The ink spelling out $14,000 on it seemed to make it feel heavier than it should have been.

Ashley was back at the Martins' house with the kids. I knew I had to call her as soon as possible to tell her what Fred had said about the piano. She thought I was lying when I told her the news. "There's no way," she said, shockingly. I reassured her that it was legit. The Heintzman was worth *a lot* more than we thought. I described Fred and my interaction in detail, including the piece of carbon paper that I was holding. "Well, what do we do now?" she asked. "I guess I'll call John," I replied.

We were less than twenty-four hours away from the house being ripped down to the studs. I needed to make arrangements for the piano one way or the other. There was a fork in the road, and time was of the essence. The Heintzman would either be absorbed by the bureaucracy of corporate America or be adopted for a season into the care of the mysterious Fred Brown. I had no idea which way it would go. I took a picture of the carbon paper and texted it to John Longfellow and followed up with an immediate phone call. "Wow," he responded, and was just as surprised as we were by the news. "This is pretty extreme," he remarked. "I've seen a few of these situations play out, and they generally don't go the way the insured party wants them to. But, hey, you have not because you ask not." The words sounded familiar to me.

John agreed to present Fred's proposal on our behalf, but he was clear in his communication about what our chances were. I said I understood and thanked him for his help. I walked over to the Heintzman and put my shoulder on it. The old wheels squeaked as I inched it toward the garage door. I wanted to avoid it being in the way of the crew that was coming to work on the house the next day. It had already experienced its fair share of trauma. I didn't want it to be kicked when it was down. I pushed it back into the corner and found whatever soft goods I could to protect it. I placed old drop cloths and packing blankets in a pile on the garage floor in front of the piano and began to put them one by one over the water-stained wood finish. As I tucked them around the corners of the cabinet, something odd crept into my thoughts. At first, I didn't recognize it. It felt foreign to me. Eventually, I came to realize whatever it was felt a little like hope. It was paralyzing. I didn't want to admit to myself that I had allowed my mind to drift in that direction. It felt irresponsible. After all, I was looking at destruction. It was right there in front of me. My inner man seized up in defense. I did my best not to let it move from my head to my heart by building a barricade with the lump in my throat.

We had been in a season characterized by death. The death of relationships, the death of dreams, and my dad's passing. We were stuck in a rut, and it was dark and deep. It had been a long time since we had given the light and buoyant air of hope permission to be felt. It's not that it wasn't out there. I'm sure that it was. It's just that the thought of nurturing hope in our innermost places felt too dangerous to entertain. What if it were misused or misplaced? What if what's hoped for never comes to fruition . . . if it's deferred? What if it all turns out to be unicorns and fairy dust? I'd be sicker than I was already.

I walked outside, entered the garage code on the keypad, and pressed enter. The garage door creaked downward behind me and came to a loud and abrupt halt when it reached the cement floor. I heard the sound echo down the street through the leaves of the oak trees. I turned and saw the rusted dumpster and storage pods in the driveway. They were a garrison standing guard. I acknowledged them silently as I walked down the driveway, leaving the Heintzman behind, deconstructed and in the dark.

I got in the car and made the drive down the street, then turned toward the Martins. At about the halfway point, a realization dawned on me. The Olsons were vagabonds. Wanderers. We were living on the daily bread of the borrowed loft and red duvet covers at the top of the narrow staircase and the nightly conversations with Joby and Gretchen after the kids went to bed. The thing was, it was exactly what we needed, and surprisingly, it was more than enough. We had no grand ten-year plan. No ambition to construct a preferred reality for ourselves. The truth is, we had no resources (or energy) to do it. We didn't even have shingles on our roof. All we could do was engage in the everyday that was right in front of us. We put one foot in front of the other, each day unfolding to the next, taking on the tasks at hand.

We changed diapers and folded laundry. We gave our kids baths in the ensuite bathroom upstairs. We made meals and washed dishes. There was a subtle sacredness of the ordinary in it. I lead worship at church. Joby preached. We got to watch God work at the altar benches at the front of the church on the weekends. It continued to be healing for me. We came back home after Sunday and set the grill on fire while we watched baseball and drank Miller Lite in the backyard. Occasionally, somebody would say something that would make everyone break out laughing. It wasn't uncommon with Joby around. It was always unplanned. Spontaneous. When it happened, I noticed it. I looked around and saw the smiles and heard the laughter. Grown-ups and kids (some grown-ups acting like kids) alike, sitting out in the sunlit backyard with the Braves play-by-play carrying on faintly in the background. Surrounded by simple things like potato chips, hamburger buns, and sliced watermelon. The sight and sound of it all slowed things down in my soul. As it unfolded, I gradually sensed the adrenaline surges and frenetic pace of dealing with one crisis after another, being politely introduced to something new and different. The two had to look each other in the eye, shake hands, and come to terms with one another.

It sounds strange, but I could actually feel the chemicals in my brain shift. Things felt softer and lighter. Some of the heaviness that had made my brow furrow began to lift. Occasionally, I even caught the corners of my mouth starting to fight the gravity that was weighing them down. None of this was immediate. It didn't even feel permanent. At this point, not much had changed circumstantially. We were still vagabonds, sleeping in borrowed beds. But there, in a house we didn't own, opened to us by people we had only recently met, I could sense something changing for the first time in a long time. Things were still foreign, but they weren't fearful.

Parallel to this came another realization. This new sense of grace could only be found in the presence of pain, not in its avoidance. Things had been painful. I had done things to make them even more painful, tripping over my own feet as I stumbled forward. Breaking things because of my broken heart. It all had worked to find us where we were. We were in the valley.

I knew about the valley. I had grown up hearing people talk about it under the A-frame. I had experienced it in the brokenness of home in my formative years. Down in its dark shadows, I lost some of the innocence of boyhood. Ironically, leaving the Phoenix desert felt like the valley too. No one wants to be in the valley. But what I was discovering was that I wasn't alone in it. God was there too, using it to do extraordinary things. As it turns out, the valley is where you discover who you really are, and who you're not. God reveals it to you as he reveals himself to you. In the valley, you look down, surprised to find yourself dressed like the vagabond, the wanderer. It's where you come to terms with the fact that your pockets are indeed empty. Things you depended on to prop yourself up have shorted out and burnt down, leaving you standing in the ashes.

The valley is a terrible and beautiful place. Some people spend their whole lives looking for what can only be found there, but they avoid it like the plague. Folks can build massive fortresses of self-preservation only to spend their lives trapped behind the walls. They become so self-reliant that they never reach the point where the water is too deep to touch the bottom. Ironically, that's the only place where what they are looking for can be found. And it's not a thing. It's a Person. On the other hand, some people find themselves in the valley, wondering how they got there. Eventually, they discover that they're not alone as they walk through it. The One they are with brought them there on purpose and with love. After poking around in that valley for a while, they end up finding that the treasure is the One walking with them.

Something was changing, and it was happening right under our noses. While we were slowing down and healing at the Martins' home, our Jacksonville house was under siege just around the corner. The blue tarp had been removed, folded up neatly, and placed in the garage. In its place, a crew of ten worked on the roof with pitchforks, prying up the old storm-damaged shingles and tossing them en masse into the dumpster that sat on the driveway below. Simultaneously, another crew was inside the house ripping up the old floors. The water-damaged builder-grade tile, carpet, and hardwood were being carted out by wheelbarrow loads into the same dumpster. All of Miss Robin's quirky home décor—gone. The wallpaper didn't stand a chance. The workers went right to the drywall, prying it away from the studs. It would all be replaced with materials approved under the renovation budget by Ashley and me, all with Father Longfellow's stamp of approval.

There was so much demolition happening that the dumpster eventually hit its limit. Someone had to call for backup. The Waldrons, who had taken Bentley in during the melee of the flood, had a front row seat. They were kind to send us updates by way of pictures over text as we sat around the dinner table at the Martins down the street. We followed up with daily visits in the afternoons to take it all in. Old toilets and sinks, insulation and carpet padding, shower heads and bathtubs, were carted off into the sea of forgetfulness. In its place, new sheets of fresh drywall, ornate crown molding, and boxes of that new sheik ceramic wood-look tile flooring were being dropped off by the truckloads. Those wide plank-looking tiles in the neutral greige color that everybody loves. The interior would get a fresh coat of paint to match. It was being loaded into the house through every door.

Ashley and I stopped by from time to time. When we did, we stood there, watching in utter disbelief. Not long before, I had held her as the water dripping from the ceiling merged with the tears on her cheeks in the front room. Now we stood in the front room experiencing a weight of a different kind. The realization of restoration. The house had regained a pulse. Eccentric tradesmen and women were buzzing around and above it. People whom we had never met were fitting pipes and mudding walls. The sound of nail guns echoed throughout the place from the crew securing the new shingles on the roof. There was so much going on that it was difficult to keep track of it all.

Something else was transpiring at the same time. John Longfellow had presented all the details about the Heintzman to the suits at the insurance company. I wasn't there to hear exactly what was said, but whatever it was lit a fire. Fred Brown's handwritten report of the piano's monetary value found its way onto someone's desk at the office. Like a mustard seed, it took root in the hard earth of the bottom-line system. In a short time, the roots began to grow. They eventually grew so large that they butted up against the actuarial algorithms of the insurance company. Before long, the Heintzman found its way into a boardroom conversation. Men in dark suits looked at white pieces of paper with numbers on them. They talked about what was in the best interest of the shareholders. I like to think things got heated, but I wasn't there for that one either. I can guarantee this, due diligence was done, and numbers were crunched. In the end, Fred's proposal won the day. It turns out that the Heintzman was worth so much money that the bureaucracy decided to fully fund its complete restoration, amounting to all $14,000. Apparently, it was cheaper than buying us out.

John called with the news. As I listened to his voice on the phone, a deeper sense of what I had felt over burgers and Miller Lite at the Martins came over me. This time, it included a mental picture of Goldy Reid's face, cracking a giant smile. The wrinkles around his eyes deepened as his cheeks pressed upward at the thought of the piano restored. In my mind, it was as if the joy he had experienced when he moved it into the Chatham house for Ashley's mom as a little girl was showering down through the generations, snowballing with each successive year. I told Ashley the news. She was dumbfounded. I saw a glimmer of light shoot up from her heart through her deep brown eyes. That tender part of her heart, so beautifully nurtured by her parents and their parents before them, began to show.

Fred was glad for the work. He showed up at the house a few days later with a box truck, some work gloves, and one of those pro piano dollies. The kind with thick ratchet straps for keeping things secure. It was midafternoon, and the western sunlight was beaming down through the oak trees that lined the street in front of the house. I greeted him at the end of the driveway as he pulled his long legs down from the truck door. We shook hands. There was a mysterious look in his eye. I gathered that he shared our disbelief that the insurance company had agreed to what we were about to do. I walked him up the driveway to the garage door and entered the code on the numeric pad. The motor purred as the door crept open, allowing the western sunlight in. The Heintzman sat back in the corner in silence, where I had left it. It was still wrapped snuggly in the packing blankets. At this point, the garage was filled with power tools and construction supplies from the renovation, and a layer of white dust covered everything from the drywall mud that had been sanded down. Fred and I made our way through the obstacles in the garage toward the piano. He grabbed the end of one of the packing blankets and pulled it back, revealing the old, murky walnut finish.

"This will be quite the project," Fred said in his wispy voice. "Yup." I was unsure how to respond. I had no way of seeing all that he was seeing. He gently tucked the blanket back around the piano. We cleared a path through the garage. Pulling on his work gloves, he wheeled the dolly from the back of the truck. We lifted the soundboard side up onto the flat part of the dolly. We could hear the echo of the soundboard as it dropped back down on the ground beneath the dampening blankets. The thick ratchet straps were secured around the piano. I helped Fred lean its weight back on the dolly and guide it down the gentle slope of the driveway to the platform of the hydraulic lift at the back of the box truck. We both worked together to muscle the weight on the platform. I stepped off as Fred reached down and pulled the lever to activate the lift. Fred and the Heintzman ascended upward off the ground as I stood on the street watching. When the lift had run its course, Fred maneuvered the piano to the inmost part of the box truck and strapped it snugly against the back wall. He slowly and cautiously climbed down to street level. After taking off his gloves, he reached out and shook my hand again. "This will take a while," he said. I nodded in response. "I'll have lots of questions." "Ok," I said. I wasn't sure what he was alluding to, but my curiosity was stirred.

Fred gingerly climbed back into the driver's side seat of the truck and shut the door. As he cranked the diesel engine, he leaned out the open window and said, "I'll call you," over the rumble. The window was rolled up, and the steering wheel was cranked to make the sharp turn out of the cul-de-sac. I stood at the end of the driveway in the afternoon sun as he and the Heintzman disappeared around the shallow curve in the road.

True to fashion, the renovation of the Jacksonville house stretched from three weeks to four. The Martins graciously kept their door open to us for an additional week. By the end of it, they swore that they didn't want us to leave. They even seemed sincere about it. We were indebted to them for providing a place to lay our heads, but more so for the time we were able to share together and the way God used it to settle us down and to heal us. I was particularly grateful for the late-night conversations in the living room with Joby and the insight they gave into pastoral life.

The night before we were allowed to move back into our place, we shared one last meal. The last supper. The stories and smiles exchanged over the table that night did the same thing in us that the previous ones had. There were smiles and stories, laughter, and love. They were a soothing balm on our fragile hearts.

CHAPTER 17

All five of the Olsons made the short drive home to the Jacksonville house. As we pulled around the shallow curve, it came into view under the oak trees that stretched over the street. The older boys pushed themselves up as far as they could from the backseat toward the windshield to take it in. Their little arms jutted up into the gap between us in the front, as their fingers pointed at what they saw. The exterior of the house was in the process of being repainted. Three house painters, wearing white jumpsuits splattered with the chosen color, hung on ladders around the house. Each was armed with a small airbrush-like paint gun, which they swung back and forth in smooth, even motion to achieve coverage over the rough cat stucco finish. The technique seemed more Picasso to me than it did Sherwin-Williams, and the house bore witness to the same. It looked like a work of art. I thought of Mr. Fun and how proud he would be when he saw it for the first time. The front was nearly completed in crisp grey and white.

Just above the ladder line sat the brand-new roof that John had negotiated for us. Up to that point in my life, I hadn't had much time for shingles, but I couldn't help but admire these. They sat in perfect formation over the cascading roofline of the house, row by row. They were a classy, deep charcoal that complemented the paint color. The eaves of the house were decked with a sharp, black metallic flashing that made their outline pop against the texture of the shingles and the bright white trim. The dumpster had been removed from the driveway. Only the storage units remained, and workers were loading the furniture that had been stored inside through the front door of the house. Before the car had come to a full stop in the driveway, the back doors flung open. Brody and Bentley took off like a shot to take in the rest of the exterior of the house. They yelled out, "Look! Look!" as they went.

John met us in the driveway. His yellow legal pad sat in his right hand with a roll of blue painter's tape. I could see the notation of the work that had already been done, as well as things that were in the process of completion. He'd use the tape to mark them. His face held a look of confident satisfaction. Ashley and I climbed out of the car to meet him. He smiled and said, "Big day." We smiled back as our eyes poured over the transformation of the outside of the house. We couldn't help but feel like we were on one of those surprise home makeovers on HGTV. John was the benevolent host, and we were the unsuspecting homeowners about ready to take it all in.

Chapter 17

We tried to stay out of the way of the workers loading the furniture as we walked toward the front door. Upon entrance, we were overcome with astonishment. It was mid-morning, and the warm Florida sunshine beamed through the large bay window as it always had. It was the same sun that I had stared into as I lay flat on my back at the end of the driveway after struggling to turn the water valve off with the wrench and screwdriver. I remember feeling the sun owed me something that day. I had been acting like it revolved around me, and I recalled my indignation that it hadn't responded the way I wanted it to. Now, as Ashley and I looked around the front room, I realized that while the sun had been at its post, stalwart in the bright blue Florida sky, things had been shifting and changing in our world below. The first thing I noticed was the scent. When we had purchased the home from Miss Robin a few months prior, it had a staleness to it. The house had been well-loved through the years, as she and her husband, Jerry, had raised their family there. However, most of the rooms in the place had been largely unused as her kids had moved away and Jerry had passed. The flood had only made things worse, adding notes of dank mildew and moisture. The air in the house was now vibrant and energetic. It was crisp, clean, and new. The new scent was emanating from all the restoration that had been done.

When we had left a month prior, the walls in the front room had been gutted, exposing the studs and electrical work. Now the house was full of new, freshly painted drywall. There was no wallpaper to be seen. The ceiling from which the water from the upstairs bathroom had poured had been replaced and retextured, complete with the ornate crown molding that had been there previously. The new wood-look ceramic tile floors ran throughout with pristine grout lines in between. The sound of the workers loading the furniture resonated through the house on the hard surface.

Ashley and I looked at John. He stood, his nose down in his yellow legal pad, comparing what he saw with the notes he had made, making sure all was as it should be. He meandered off into the kitchen to continue his work. I left Ashley and walked over to the staircase where the conversation had happened after my dad's funeral. The one that had led to the flood. Looking down, I noticed that the carpet running up the stairs had been replaced. I took my shoes off and climbed the stairs that I had sprinted up, three and four at a time, with the bucket for Ashley, and turned the corner toward the bathroom. As I walked in, I was confronted with all that had been done since I had channeled my inner turmoil down through my hands onto the old vanity. The bathtub that Ashley had tried to divert the water from the broken pipes had been replaced by a subway tile shower with a beautiful glass door. The floors of the bathroom, which had been completely doused in water, now matched the new ones on the first floor. Those walls had been gutted out and replaced as well. And there, directly in front of me, was a new stand-alone vanity with a bright white granite countertop and dark bronze fixtures to match the ones in the adjoining shower.

I was silent. I didn't know how to process it. Part of me wanted to cry, part of me wanted to chuckle. It was as I had wanted it to be for my brother-in-law's arrival. But I had done nothing, save the accident, to get it that way. I heard Brody and Bentley come in the front door downstairs. Their footsteps echoed off the floor downstairs as they ran around in excitement. I pulled myself away from the sight of the new vanity and walked back down the stairs. Ashley was helping the workers arrange the furniture as they moved it in.

John walked around the corner from the kitchen into the front room. "Well," he said. "I think we're in good shape. I have a line of sight on the things that need to be done yet. It's not much. Thank you, guys, for your flexibility with the construction delays. These things rarely go as planned." I laughed. He continued, "Quite a transformation. The roof is done. They'll be done with the paint job out there today. Pretty much everything in here is good to go." He handed me the roll of blue painter's tape. "If you see anything that needs attention, mark it with this and the contractor will make sure it's looked after," he noted. "On the money side, things are pretty much buttoned up as well. Materials and labor for the roof and interior renovation are all squared away. There are only a few things that need to be worked through yet. Most of those have to do with your personal possessions." We both turned and glanced at the empty spot on the wall by the bay window where the Heintzman once sat. "Yup," he said. "I still can't believe they bit on that. It's my understanding that it's going to take Fred quite a while to finish. Once he's done, I'll work with you to get it squared away with the insurance company."

Ashley and I walked John to the front door. "I'd prefer not to see you guys again," he said. Ashley and I laughed as our eyes dropped to the floor. He smiled in return. I reached out to shake his hand. As I did, I remembered climbing up on the roof with the blue tarp and bags of topsoil after Matthew had moved through. I also remembered the hopelessness that had pinned me down as we were caught between the HOA and the insurance company. All of that, and so much more, had since been resolved, and Father Longfellow had been our advocate in it all. Monetarily speaking, he would be compensated by a small percentage of the claims that he had negotiated on our behalf. We felt we owed him much more. Whether he knew it or not, he had been instrumental in God's restorative work in the life of our family. It wasn't just the roof, the walls, and the floors. I wanted him to know it, but the words got caught in my throat. I looked him in the eye one last time before he turned away. "I'll be in touch," he said.

The Olsons spent the afternoon getting reacquainted with the Jacksonville house in its new state. The belongings that had seen us through the month with the Martins found their way from the old, road-worn luggage back into the closets in each respective room. The boys loved the feel of the new carpet on their bare feet in their upstairs rooms and the fancy glass shower door in the renovated bathroom. Beckett's nursery furniture had been loaded back in. That night, he would make the jump from the pack n' play in the closet back to his crib. I made sure the TV and stereo were all wired up in the living room while Ashley made a trip to the grocery store to fill the empty refrigerator. That evening, after the workers left, we sat around our own kitchen table and had a home-cooked meal together under a brand-new roof.

I enjoyed spending the early morning hours in the front room. There was a small chair and a side table that faced east toward the bay window. Most mornings, I would find myself sitting in that chair in the faint pre-dawn light. Ashley and the kids would still be asleep, as at that time of the year the sun rose later than it did in the summer months. I kept my Bible on the table next to the chair. I would sit with it open on my lap while the sun came up over the pine trees that lined the fairway behind the house.

On clear days, I would watch the sky gradually slide from deep blues and violets to pale pinks and oranges. There would often be a brief and wonderful moment when an ornate texture would materialize on the surface of the clouds in rich carnation pink as the sun, not yet cresting over the horizon, would catch them. It was as if they were giving a hint at what was to come. After that moment had run its course, the texture would fade into a broader orange glow. In my mind, I knew the science. The earth was spinning around the sun at a steady pace, never slowing down and never speeding up, just as it had since it was created. Those mornings led me to doubt the math. Seemingly all at once, the orange glow would swell in intensity as the saffron gleam of the sun would burst through the pine branches. It evoked the feeling that the rotation of the earth sped up excitedly as the sky gave birth to the sun's light. It was resplendent and glorious.

Eventually, the morning light would creep in through the bay window and cast its warmth on the freshly painted walls of the front room. The words on the pages of my Bible that were once undiscernible in the twilight of the predawn were illuminated. My attention drifted down from the horizon to the stories on the pages below. Story after story, each giving a glimpse into God's heart. There was Sarah, who bore the child of promise when she was as good as dead. Then Elijah, who spread his body over the lifeless corpse of the Shunammite woman's son, and the peculiarity of the seven sneezes that preceded the blinking of his eyes. Ezekiel's valley of dry bones took on sinews and flesh, while his prophecy to the breath and the life of the exceedingly great army followed. There were the triumphant words of Isaiah:

> *And he will swallow up on this mountain the covering that is cast over all peoples, the veil that is spread over all nations. He will swallow up death forever; and the Lord God will wipe away tears from all faces, and the reproach of his people he will take away from all the earth, for the Lord has spoken.*
>
> (Isaiah 25:7-8)

The story of Lazarus, alive and reclining at the Bethany table, and the fragrance of gratitude that filled the room. There was a vacant tomb of a rich man named Joseph from the town of Arimathea, and Jesus's words of fire on the Emmaus Road.

I drank in the words, letting them find a home in my heart. I stretched to put myself in the place of each character, imagining the most minute details. The sights, sounds, and smells. I zoomed out to 50,000 feet and tried to wrap my mind around the bigness of the story, asking myself important questions. What was God up to? What was He trying to convey as He was mysteriously working through both the miraculous and mundane? His Spirit moved steadily and faithfully down through the ages to where I sat in the small chair in front of the bay window.

Morning after morning, the sun rose, and I read. And every morning, there was a conspicuously vacant spot on the wall to my right. It was the front room wall adjacent to the bay window, just underneath the upstairs bathroom, where the Heintzman used to sit. The bareness of it made the room feel lopsided and uncomfortable.

Over the course of the weeks that followed, I would receive calls at random times from Fred Brown. They were always impromptu and unscheduled. When I saw his name on my phone, I would prioritize answering the call, ducking out of church meetings during workdays. I was always glad to hear his faint voice on the other side of the line. After a few minutes of catching up over casual conversation, he would ask questions. The questions always struck me as cryptic. I knew that he was at work. When he had pulled away with the Heintzman in the back of the box truck, we had a mutual understanding that he would restore the piano and that the process would be very involved. But I had no idea of the specifics of what he was doing. I didn't know the order in which the restoration needed to take place. What needed to be addressed first? I didn't know where one would find the parts and pieces needed for the job. The felt and hammers, and the small pieces of canvas that connected the keys to them. Come to think of it, I didn't even know where he (or the Heintzman) was. I had no physical address. I didn't know if he had a shop he worked in or if he worked from his home. Yet I could tell from the questions that he was up to something.

Fred asked, "Michael, what do you want this thing to look like?" It was the first time that I realized that I had a choice. I thought about the murky walnut finish that I had buried beneath the packing blankets in the garage. I remembered the stains where the water had penetrated the worn-out lacquer on the top of the cabinet. I considered the options.

"Can you make it look like it did when it was brand new?" I responded. There was a brief pause. In the silence, I could tell that Fred was visualizing what something like that would entail. I pictured Fred stripping the old uneven lacquer from the body of the Heintzman, exposing the natural grain of the walnut to the open air. I pictured him sanding down the imperfections by hand, bringing everything to an even place. It would be a long and tedious job. All the ornate places around the legs that couldn't be reached with power tools would need to be addressed. I visualized him dropping his lips down to the wood's surface and blowing away the sawdust as he worked. I saw him holding a series of color swatches up in the daylight and looking at them each intently through his readers. He imagined what the piano must have looked like in the early 1900s in the Heintzman showroom somewhere on the outskirts of Toronto. Breaking the silence, he said, "Yes, I believe I can."

A few weeks later, he called again. "Michael, what do you want this thing to sound like?" Again, I realized that I hadn't thought through the depth and complexity involved in what he was doing. "What do you mean?" I responded. "Well, do you want it to be bright? Do you want it to sound like a Yamaha or a Kawai? Like a Japanese make? Or do you want it to be more European-sounding?" He rattled off his questions. I knew about Yamaha pianos. I remembered the one I grew up with in the front room of the Elmhurst house. The one that ended up in the consignment shop after my parents' divorce. I loved that piano and had wanted it at one point. My siblings and I were sad about where it ended up and how it had gotten there, but that seemed so long ago.

I thought about the opportunity in front of me. Fred's questions led me to believe that it was possible to get the Heintzman to sound like the one I grew up with. For a moment, the thought had a sense of appeal to it, but I knew it wasn't right. The Heintzman was a different kind of instrument. It had come from a different place, and it wasn't going in the same direction. I didn't want to waste this opportunity trying to make it something it was never meant to be. I asked Fred, "What do European pianos sound like?" "Well, generally speaking, they are a bit darker. Japanese pianos tend to be bright. You know, more forward. European pianos are different. In my opinion, they have more character," he shared.

The word *character* jumped out in my mind. "It's all in the hammers and the felt, really," he continued. "The European felt is softer. When it hits the strings, it comes off warmer to the ear." I thought about it for a moment. The Heintzman was over a century old. It had made its way from Toronto to Chatham. From Chatham to London. From London to Nashville. From Nashville to Phoenix, and from Phoenix to Jacksonville, where all hell had broken loose over its head. *Character*! Yes, if it needed to retain anything, it would be a sense of character. That unique sense about a thing that tells you where it's been and what it's been through. I tried to imagine a version of the Heintzman that had been completely restored from the inside out and still retained a unique sense of character. The more I thought about it, the more appealing it became. I tried to describe what was in my mind to Fred. I'm not sure it all came out the way I wanted it to, and I was afraid of what would happen if it didn't. But after I was done, he said, "European," and hung up the phone.

After that conversation, I didn't hear from Fred for quite a while. Our attention shifted to the everyday. Things fell into place at the Jacksonville house as we got back into the rhythms of family life. Eventually, all the new in the place started to feel like us. I stopped thinking as much about the pipe's bursting when I helped the kids brush their teeth at the sink in the upstairs bathroom. The memory of all of Miss Robin's eclectic home décor choices started to fade with each passing day. Brody and Bentley went to school. I began to get my bearings at Eleven22. It was a hectic phase for Ashley and me, changing diapers and chasing the kids around at home. Not to mention my own efforts to keep up with the rapid pace of growth at the church. The thought of the Heintzman being over at Fred's never left my mind, but it did drift more to the back as more pressing things took precedence. Occasionally, when I would sit with my Bible in the front room and watch the sunrise, I would have a surge of curiosity about how things were going, but I never reached out to check in. For some reason, that felt like holding on to things too tightly.

Six months after watching Fred drive away with the piano in the back of the box truck, I saw his name pop up on my cell phone. When it did, I knew what he was calling about. He told me he had finished the job, and he was asking if there was a convenient time to drop the Heintzman off at the house. I stopped and noticed my reaction to his words. Part of me expected some immediate elation. What happened was different. I felt a restrained anticipation in my stomach. My muscles tightened as if I was bracing myself for impact. An overly extroverted, petty sort of happiness didn't suit this kind of news. That sort of happiness might follow much later, in the wake of the deeper work that was being done, but to rush into it would be to miss the significance. Also, I knew this phone call was bound to come. In a way, I expected it, but oddly, there was still an element of surprise when it did. Fred was short and to the point. We mutually agreed on a date and time for the delivery. After I hung up the phone, I told Ashley. She had the same reaction that I did.

The day of the delivery, Fred showed up in the same box truck that he had used to pick up the Heintzman six months prior. All five of the Olsons stood huddled in waiting at the front door. The truck let out a loud series of beeps as he backed into the driveway. We all went out to meet him. Taking his hands to the latch at the door's bottom, Fred heaved upward, shoving the sliding door open. It shot upward and landed with a loud jolt. Ashley and I peered into the darkness in front of us, trying to catch a glimpse of whatever was inside. We saw the shape of the Heintzman covered again in dark blue packing blankets, strapped to the back wall of the truck. Fred climbed in, quickly loosened the ratchet straps, and grabbed the dolly. I climbed up into the back of the truck to give him a hand.

After securing the piano to the dolly, we worked it back onto the platform of the hydraulic lift much as we had done before. Ashley and the boys stood on the ground, watching as Fred threw the switch. Fred, the covered Heintzman, and I slowly descended to the driveway. Fred braced himself, pulled the weight of the brass soundboard back on the dolly, positioned the wheels toward the front door, and began to move forward. When we arrived, I helped him lift the Heintzman off the dolly and over the threshold into the front room. Once inside, Fred paused for a moment to collect himself. He lifted his eyes up and looked around. "Wow," he said in between breaths. "This place looks different." I realized the last time Fred had seen the Jacksonville house, it was days into being renovated. "Yeah, a lot has happened in here since you've seen it last," I replied. "I'm glad," he said, "'cause it was kind of a mess."

Ashley and I laughed. Fred and I took our hands to the piano. The wheels glided easily over the new porcelain tile floors as we pushed it from the doorway into the vacant spot on the wall adjacent to the bay window. Ashley stood back and directed us as we brought it to the center. A little to the left, a little to the right. When it found its place, I stepped away to take it in before it was unwrapped. To the eye, it looked like nothing at all. A pile of blue blankets. They hung about the frame like the burial garments used to protect the dead, old, and ragged. A few months ago, that was what they were. But there was something mysteriously glorious that was about to be unveiled just under the surface.

Fred and I began to peel the blankets back from the piano one at a time until what he had been working on in secret was fully and finally revealed. As they rustled, the tightness in my muscles that I had experienced during the phone call grew. When the last blanket hit the floor, I turned to look at Ashley's reaction. Soft tears began to well up in the inside corners of her beautiful brown eyes as she stood in the middle of the room, looking at what Fred had done. It was as if she could see her mother as a little girl sitting on the bench in the Chatham house. It made the little girl in her come alive. Some of the layers of self-defense she had built to weather the loss were washing away down her cheeks as she embraced the moment.

I shifted my attention to Fred, who had stepped back himself to take it in. He stared at the work of his hands with steady admiration as it shone in the daylight streaming through the bay window. He was reliving the journey he had been on with the Heintzman over the last six months. He crossed his arms and cocked his head as a subtle grin crept over his face. I stepped back, took my turn, and saw for myself what elicited their response.

The old, dead, murky walnut finish, which I had wrapped with the blue packing blankets, was now alive in vivid detail. The delicate grain of the wood that had once been hidden by the years and the miles had been rediscovered. It was like an ancient treasure that Fred had hunted down. The movement of the grain swirled and curled over the body of the piano like a work of high art crafted by the fingers of God himself. It was beautiful. I was naturally drawn to the panel directly over the keys that covered the action. I stared at it as if it were a Van Gogh in the Louvre, my eye drawn to each stroke of the artist's brush. The intentionality and attention to detail of the original craftsman became clear, and Ashley and I saw it for the first time. He had chosen the most striking piece of walnut and reserved it for the most visible location. Cutting it in perfect symmetry, he created a regal book-matched finish whose seam ran right down the middle. It was royal, like the ornate regalia of a king. I couldn't believe my eyes. "That was under there the entire time," Fred said. "You just couldn't see it."

After taking in the finish on the outside, Fred lifted the book-matched front panel off and gently set it aside, exposing the work he had done inside. It was beautifully intricate. A look into the mind of a brilliant pre-industrial revolution musical engineer, but it was reborn. The old wooden hammers that had yellowed over the years had been replaced with brand new ones. Their color was younger. More neutral and pale. Each hammer was donned precisely with bright white felt surrounded by crimson red trim. They looked like soldiers standing at attention outside Buckingham Palace. The small canvas strips that attached the keys to the action lay in a perfect row, each with the same crimson detail on its tip.

Fred grabbed the bench, pulled it in front of the piano, and lifted the cover, revealing the keys. As I looked down, I recognized them as original, but many of the chips and ridges that they had borne previously had been filed down or filled in. *Character*, I thought. Fred had understood what I had said. "Go ahead," he said, gesturing with his palm to the open bench. I looked at Ashley. She wiped a tear from her eye, nodded, and smiled. I remembered my dad on the organ bench in the front room of the Elmhurst house. In much the same way, I slid onto the bench and brought my fingers to the keys. The last time I saw them, most were lifeless, unable to pick themselves up after drowning in the flood. Now they stood at attention, rigid and alert. I inched my index finger to the middle of the keyboard and started with a single note. As I compressed the key, the beautiful machine in front of me sprang into action. The canvas pulled the wooden dowel attached to the hammer. The hammer moved forward perfectly, its timing perfectly synchronized. The felt on the end of the hammer struck the shiny new steel string, which resonated through the original brass soundboard that stood vertically against the back wall. The result was a beautiful, pure tone, warm to the ear.

"European," Fred said, standing over my shoulder. I slowly brought the rest of my hands into play, shaping chords just as my dad had at the organ on the right under the old A-frame. One note led to two. Two led to six . . . and then seven. The strong octaves in the left hand were supporting colorful harmony in the right. I moved through the chordal structure, improvising as I went. Music began to spill from my heart down through my fingers. Eventually, the front room was full of the most beautiful sound. It echoed off the new porcelain floors and the glass of the bay window much as it had underneath the skylight in the red room the night before our wedding. It reminded me of the sound of the organ under the A-frame. The boys ran in from the kitchen, summoned by the sound. They listened as I spoke the language that my father had taught me so many years before. The sound surrounded them. It hemmed them in. While I played, I looked in their direction. I could see a glimmer in each of their eyes, a tell-tale sign of a connection being made down in the deepest parts of their young, innocent hearts. I recognized it. It reminded me of the way I felt as I wept under the staircase at Northwest Assembly as a little boy.

As I sat on the bench, I thought of some of the words that had been illuminated by the morning light streaming through the bay window.

> *Truly, truly, I say to you, you will weep and lament, but the world will rejoice. You will be sorrowful, but your sorrow will turn into joy. When a woman is giving birth, she has sorrow because her hour has come, but when she has delivered the baby, she no longer remembers the anguish, for joy that a human*

> *being has been born into the world. So also you have sorrow now, but I will see you again, and your hearts will rejoice, and no one will take your joy from you. In that day you will ask nothing of me. Truly, truly, I say to you, whatever you ask of the Father in my name, he will give it to you. Until now you asked nothing in my name. Ask, and you will receive, that your joy may be full.* (John 16:20-24)

There, in the reborn and renovated front room of the Jacksonville house, as the music resounded from the Heintzman, I understood what Jesus was talking about. *Resurrection.* Life incorruptible. The kind that makes a mockery of death, swallowing it up and making it a means to a greater and more glorious end. It is not the absence of sorrow; it is sorrow redeemed. It is sorrow that gives purpose and meaning. It is not the absence of death; it is the glorious life that one discovers on the other side of it. The kind of life that comes with the authority to ask bold questions and pray bold prayers for the increase of joy.

It's true. The organ under the A-Frame had shorted out and burnt our church home to the ground. I saw the ashes smolder with my own eyes. It's also true that my dad's beautiful heart was hijacked by a diabolical enemy. He spent decades of his life enslaved to jealousy, envy, and rage. I saw the demons at work, poking and prodding him in the tense silence around the family dinner table. I hated it. I also saw him fight as hard as he could at the organ bench in the front room. He fought the only way he knew how and, seemingly, it wasn't enough. He shorted out too.

I saw his lifeless body lying cold and quiet in a casket at the funeral home.

But . . .

These days, at just the right time when I climb the side steps up to the piano as Joby is turning the corner toward the close of his sermon . . . after I push all the right buttons and turn all the right nobs, and my hands drift down to the keys in front of me . . . the first thing I think about is my dad. As you now know, I came by the spot behind those keys honestly, and most of that has to do with him. As the music moves from my heart to my fingers, I have an inescapable sense that he is with me, looking over my shoulder. He nods in sweet approval as the sound fills the room. "That's it, son," he says softly. "Just like that."

His affirmation hits my heart like rain in the desert, filtering into the deepest parts of who I am. It makes me smile as I play. His elder brother, Jesus, stands behind him, showering him with the same affectionate admiration. He is the source; the depth of the well of His unconditional love cannot be fathomed. His scarred hand rests on my dad's shoulder, proof of the price of resurrection paid. My dad's beautifully deep soul is reborn and clad in the power of Christ's indestructible life. He is now spirit in the Spirit, but he is awaiting the fully glorified body that has been purchased for him by the same scars.

The finality of sin's curse and its consequence has been broken—snapped like the headstock of the '69 Gibson. When the lungs of Jesus began to expand in that cold, dark tomb, that curse splintered into 10,000 pieces. We are invited to live our lives in the euphoric joy of all that follows, rolling around in Spirit-born laughter as we go about our days. Relationship with God has been fully restored, and it is spilling over in glorious harmony with all that He is redeeming around us. Sometimes it's obvious, sometimes it is subtle. But it's the truth.

The thought of my dad's affirming gaze has changed things for me. It's brought a sense of shape and purpose to the pain of the journey. In Christ, I see him in a different light. I have a sense of solidarity with him, recognizing where some of my thoughts and feelings come from. Sometimes it frightens me, but the knowledge that God is lovingly at work in all things for His glorious purpose tempers the fear. In a profound way, I can see Jesus more clearly because of it. I more fully understand God's heart in the redemptive work of Christ and what He's up to in the world, and why.

I often think of my sons, Brody, Bentley, and Beckett. These beautiful blond-headed boys that God has graciously given to Ashley and me. As I write this, they are fourteen, eleven, and eight years of age, entering the years that will be the most formative in making them the men they will become. They have the same blood coursing through their veins. The same mysterious depth of soul as me and my father before me. As the days we share come and go, I wonder what they will say about me when they are older. I wonder how what I say and do will impact the way they see the world. There are aspirations that I hope to fulfill, and things that I want to do and be for each of them. Things I can't do on my own. They must be done by resurrection power in me. Some of them come from the good things my dad gave me. Some of them are reactions to what I feel like I never got. I know I won't be around forever. Someday I'll join my dad, standing with Jesus's scarred hand of affirmation on my shoulder. When that time comes and people ask them the question, "What was your dad like?" I hope they can be quick and honest in responding . . .

> *He lived life with passion. He truly loved Mom. They shared something so genuine and special. He was faithful to her until the very end. He never stopped kissing us. He prayed over us at night. He made dinners, washed dishes, and folded laundry. He came to our games and was loud in the stands, cheering us on. The dinner table was never quiet. We laughed a good bit. When he spoke about God, it was as if he knew Him . . . as if he loved Him. His knowledge of God's Word was less like spitting out Bible verses and more like a pair of glasses through which he saw the world. He made it make sense to us. He told us the truth in a loving way, even when it hurt.*

And if, in that same conversation, that person happens to ask them what their dad did for a living, I hope they say . . .

> *Well . . . Dad led the singing at church, but it was more than just singing. You see, Dad had a big soul. He loved God with it. He loved us, too. He used it to build the temples that we worshipped in as little boys. Not only us, but people by the thousands. Folks whose names we'll never know. I watched as they would react to him singing and playing. It was a sight to*

behold. But the thing is, they weren't looking at him. They were too overcome by a sense of the presence of the God he loved so much. It's like something that was dead came alive in them when he used the gifts God gave him.

I hope my boys see how important it all is—the worship of God, how much it's worth. I hope I can help them see it the way my father helped me, despite our grave imperfections. I hope they understand how that legacy has shaped them and how it can propel them forward as they live the lives God lays in front of them, wherever they may lead. And at the end of their attempt to describe how I spent my energy and passion, as they look back, I hope they're able to smile the same way I do when I think of my dad, standing with Christ's scarred hand of affirmation on his shoulder. And maybe, at the end of the conversation, when they try and sum it all up, they might say . . .

Daddy set the church on fire.

GUIDED REFLECTION

Back to John's Revelation on the Isle of Patmos. Who knows how long John had been caught up in his heavenly trance? Maybe not even John himself. It had been a journey of epic proportions, his imagination coursing with symbolic imagery. From where he sat, the deep grief he once felt looking at the sealed scroll in the King's grip felt like forever ago. After the Lamb had broken the seals, he had been ushered into all that the King had intended, and as it turns out, it was complicated. No doubt he had seen victory, but it came by way of famine, fire, and war. There had been dragonish beasts and deceptive harlots. There had even been bowls of wrath poured out by the angels themselves. But in it all, even the darkest moments, the redemptive purpose of the great King and the healed scars of the Lamb had loomed large. Babylon, the once great stronghold of evil, was now a fallen city. It had been razed to the ground. The victory had been won, but the world in which his dream had taken place had suffered a tremendous amount of collateral damage. John scanned the horizon, and all he could see was smoldering ash. Then something caught his attention. He took a closer look.

John realized that there were millions and millions of bright green shoots pushing up through the ashes. He took a long blink and squinted to make sure what he saw was real. It was very real. As real as the King himself and happening quickly. As he spun around and took it all in, he realized that the world, which had been so badly ravaged by war and fire, was now teeming with new life. There were vibrant colors, wild and eclectic sounds, and beautiful scents around every corner. The very ruins of Babylon itself were being swallowed up and overshadowed by the canopy of a grove of majestic redwoods before his very eyes. They were bursting out of the ground with gusto. The tops of the growing trees pulled his gaze skyward as they shot up. He noticed a fresh easterly wind had pushed away the dark haze which had previously filled the air. The smoky sky was now completely clear, and the air crisp and cool. He breathed it in deeply, cricking his neck upward. New stars and planets were forming overhead in real time with explosive energy. They were incalculable as they pierced through the air with brilliant hues he hadn't yet seen. John was dumbfounded. What was happening? How was all this possible? As he tried to take it all in, something began to form down in his soul. It was a kind of recollection, the feeling of something familiar. Although the more he reached for whatever that memory was, the more it became clear that it was something he hadn't yet experienced. Odd. He struggled to find words to articulate what was happening inside of him. And then a word rose up from his gut and tumbled over his lips, "Eden."

Just then, his eyes were drawn to a particular object that seemed to be descending from the heavens above to the earth below. The closer the object got, the larger it appeared. Amidst all that was happening around him, John couldn't take his eyes off the object. In a matter of just a few moments, and to his astonishment, he realized that what he was looking at was a walled city floating down gracefully from heaven to where he was standing. The colors of the city walls reminded him of what he had seen in the throne room earlier in his dream. Jasper. Carnelian. He was mesmerized as it finally touched down on the lush green earth, completely dwarfing him. As he stood staring at the city, whose gate was wide open before him, he heard a familiar voice address him personally. "Behold, I am making all things new." It was his friend, Jesus the Nazarene.

A smoldering A-frame sanctuary and a woeful Eden departure. The fractured headstock of a vintage guitar and the Lamb's authority to open the sealed scroll. A once destroyed, now fully restored, family heirloom piano in the front room, and John's vision of the new Jerusalem descending from a new heaven to a new earth. What can we take from all of this? What is it all about?

As I've looked back on the twists and turns in my own story, I've started to get a sense of something. Reaching back, I can see it in the dark confusion I felt from the loss of both my father and my boyhood home to brutal unforgiveness. I can see it in the way the spirit of that same unforgiveness reared its ugly head in my relationship with my closest friend, nearly pulling me down the same road. It was there in the power of Jesus's word breaking that spirit and ushering in a beautiful reconciliation out of the pain. At present, it's very real in the sense of approval I feel from my dad. It's just as real when I kiss the heads of each of my three sons and daily watch them grow into the men God designed them to be. In all this, here's what I've begun to recognize: *God is at work healing what's been broken in ways more creative than I can comprehend.*

Perhaps you, too, have begun to see the possibility of reconciliation and healing in places you never thought possible. You might even start to hope. Real hope is dangerous. It stands in stark contrast to all that has been (and still may be) broken in and around us. It feels illogical and costly. But hope in Jesus's willingness and ability to heal and restore what's broken in and around us is not wasted energy. Paul, in Romans, writes of a well-placed hope born of suffering which produces endurance and character. In the end, that hope "does not put us to shame" (Romans 5:5).

Maybe you are a son or daughter who has distanced yourself from the idea of a real relationship with your father out of a sense of self-preservation. Perhaps you are a mother or father who is carrying around the weight of the wound you gave your child. Both feel impassable. Maybe life has become incredibly complicated, leaving you with a deep sense of betrayal by a spouse or a close friend. Perhaps you are living life with the guilt of knowing you were the betrayer. In either case, you know it's unresolved, and now you're a million miles from seeing eye to eye. You might have even tried to fix the situation in your own power, making it worse. It is as if you are standing in a flooded house with a destroyed piano, a crowbar, and good intentions in hand. A well-placed hope—a hope in Jesus—can allow you to see where you are in the light of where

He's taking you. A restoration from the inside out is ahead. *He's making all things new*. The impact of that restoration may be felt in grander and more profound ways than you can possibly imagine.

PRAYER

Father,

It's been a long time since I've allowed myself to hope.

Opening my heart up to the idea that things could be different from what they are right now has felt too risky.

There are people that I love deeply that I've been keeping at a distance out of self-preservation.The few times I've tried to make things right on my own have backfired.

I can't do it by myself; I need your help.

I'm choosing to believe that you are at work in all this, accomplishing something bigger than I can understand or imagine.

You've said that you are making all things new.

I want to be a part of it. I ask this in the name and authority of Jesus.

Amen.

Behold, I will send you Elijah the prophet before the great and awesome day of the LORD comes. And he will turn the hearts of fathers to their children and the hearts of children to their fathers, lest I come and strike the land with a decree of utter destruction.

Malachi 4:5-6

EPILOGUE

My dad sings when he washes the dishes. He'll stand in front of the sink with his back to the rest of us, belting out some silly song that Pop taught us at the top of his lungs while scrubbing the sticky stuff off the pots and pans. He can sing incredibly high and incredibly loud. It's impossible to ignore. I swear I've heard the frames of the family photos in the hallway rattle against the wall when he's doing it. Mom, who is always standing to his left with a drying towel, usually starts giggling before she joins. Before long, all of us brothers are chiming in while putting the clean dishes away. Even Brody, who is the softest spoken of the family. I love it.

Sometimes I get up early and go with my dad to church on Sunday mornings. He has to be there before everybody else to prepare the music. He'll pull his truck up over the curb and park in the grass behind the building, so he doesn't take up a spot in the parking lot out front. It can get a little crazy out there after service is over. We always walk in through the back door, into the room with the giant couch and the snacks, before we walk up the stairs to the platform where Dad's piano sits.

Making the turn past the curtain into the room where big church happens never gets old. It's massive. It looks like a hundred-foot wall of seats shooting up from the floor. I'll run up the stairs to the very top row and pick one while Dad gets ready with the rest of the band. He'll pull his computer out, hook it up, and push a bunch of buttons to make the piano sound the way it does. I'm always curious what he's doing up there. I love listening to music from the top row. I can't quite explain it, but something happens to my heart when it starts, especially when I hear Dad's voice through those giant speakers. I think it's because I know that in just a little while, that room will be filled with people singing along with him to God. There's something about it that just feels right to me.

Every once in a while, he'll talk about Grandpa playing the organ in the church in Chicago where he grew up as a little kid. When he does, his eyes light up a little bit. My mom told me that Grandpa came to visit us in our Phoenix house after I was born, but I don't remember meeting him. Dad talks about the music Grandpa made in that church and what it did to his heart. I wonder if what happens to me in the top row is the same. I guess it probably is.

I'm fascinated by the piano in our front room at home, the old one that dad ruined when he flooded the house after we moved to Jacksonville. The one we got from Nana and Pop. It's good now. I love it when Dad lifts the front panel off it when he plays. It's louder than when it's on, and I can see the hammers hit the strings when he presses the keys. It looks like they're dancing.

My dad likes playing the old songs, the ones that he said Grandpa used to play when he was growing up. I like them, too. When no one else is around, I'll sit down on that piano bench myself. I love the echoing sound that happens when I press the pedal down, and the way the keys feel under my fingers. That piano bench is a special place to me. To be honest, I don't really know what I'm doing when I'm there, but something happens to me when I press the keys down and the sound comes out. It's like my head and my heart are holding hands. I can let my imagination go a little. I feel more alive.

The other day, when I was sure I was alone, I worked up enough courage to start singing along with the music I was making with my fingers. I've seen my dad do this thousands of times. I guess I just wanted to know what it felt like for myself. I loved it so much I nearly forgot where I was. After a few minutes, I realized that Mom and Dad were watching me from around the corner in the kitchen. I felt so embarrassed that I took my fingers off the keys as quickly as I possibly could. When I looked closer, I realized Mom had tears in her eyes. She placed her head on Dad's shoulder as he smiled and put his arm around her. Then he looked at me and said, "Keep going, son."

For more information on resources from Michael Charles Olson including the audio presentation of Daddy Set the Church on Fire: A Journey Toward Restoration and Songs of Restoration, an EP of original music inspired by the book, please visit

WWW.MICHAELCHARLESOLSON.COM